Becoming Spiritually Beautiful

Sharon Jaynes

HARVEST HOUSE PUBLISHERS
EUGENE, OREGON

Cover by Garborg Design Works, Savage, Minnesota

Cover photo © Gregory Bibikov / iStockphoto.com

BECOMING SPIRITUALLY BEAUTIFUL
Copyright © 2003/2007 by Sharon Jaynes
Published by Harvest House Publishers
Eugene, Oregon 97402
www.harvesthousepublishers.com

Library of Congress Cataloging-in-Publication Data
Jaynes, Sharon.
   [Experience the ultimate makeover]
   Becoming spiritually beautiful / by Sharon Jaynes.
      p. cm.
   Originally published: Experience the ultimate makeove. Eugene, Or. : Harvest House Publishers, c2007.
   Includes bibliographical references.
   ISBN 978-0-7369-2679-9 (pbk.)
   1. Christian women—Religious life. I. Title.
   BV4527.J395 2009
   248.8'43—dc22

                                                      2009024832

Printed in the United States of America

13 14 15 16 17 18 / VP-SK / 12 11 10 9 8 7 6 5 4

ACKNOWLEDGMENTS

God has used many people in my journey of becoming spiritually beautiful: Doril and Jack Henderson, who invested their lives in a little insecure adolescent girl; the men and women of Rocky Mount, North Carolina, who established the Ancient of Days coffeehouse when contemporary Christian music made its debut; and Mr. Don Evans, who encouraged a young teenager to stand up and tell her story. God used four people to open my eyes to the truth of who I am in Christ: authors Neil Anderson, Anabel Gillham, and Bill Gillham, and my mentor, Mary Marshall Young.

I would also like to thank the incredible team at Harvest House Publishers for their vision to encourage and equip men and women through the printed word: Bob Hawkins Sr., Bob Hawkins Jr., Terry Glaspey, Carolyn McCready, LaRae Weikert, Barb Sherrill, Kim Moore, and Betty Fletcher.

A special thanks to Liz Higgs and Carol Kent for their encouraging words, my prayer team for lifting me before God's throne, and the many women who have written to share how God has set them free and begun the ultimate makeover in their own lives.

Also, this book has my husband's fingerprints on every page. Thank you, Steve, for enduring stacks of paper, late nights with me at the computer, and, "Honey, can you read this one more time?"

Finally, I want to thank my heavenly Father for His transforming work in my own life. To God be the glory!

CONTENTS

A New Kind of Beauty

Discovering God's
Transforming Power

"What's wrong with me?" I wondered. "Why can't I have the peace in my life I see in other people? Why don't I have the faith I sense in Christians around me? Why do I always feel as though I am simply not good enough?"

For many years I was held captive by feelings of inferiority, insecurity, and inadequacy. I looked as though I had it all together on the outside, but on the inside I was a cowering little girl hiding in the corner of the playground, hoping no one would notice my reluctance to join in.

You might expect me to tell you, "But then I met Jesus and all my insecurities melted away." Oh, I wish that were the case, but the insecure lost girl grew up to become an insecure Christian woman. But I'm getting ahead of myself. Let me take you on a journey through my childhood to discover the root of my inability to experience God's peace and purpose in my life. Who knows? Maybe you'll see yourself walking the path with me.

Like many children living through the depression in rural North Carolina, my parents graduated from high school and then said "I do" at the altar a few weeks later. Ten months passed, and they heard their first baby's cry. Five years after my brother was born, I made my grand debut on a snowy night just a few days before Christmas.

From the very beginning, my parents had a rocky marriage. I don't remember much about my first five years of life, but I do remember many heated arguments and violent outbursts followed by periods of cold, passive aggression.

My father ran a building supply company and spent most of his time away from home, working or carousing with friends. And even though his place of business was only a few miles from our home, I felt that his heart was in a place I could never find. A battle raged in my little girl heart between the part of me that longed to be a daddy's girl and the part that feared to even get near him.

My family lived in a beautiful brick ranch-style home with columns on an elongated front porch and 60-foot pine trees forming a shady canopy over our roof. With two kids and a collie named Lassie, we looked like the typical all-American family. But behind the peaceful exterior loomed a deep dark secret.

My father had a drinking problem, and many nights he came home in violent fits of rage. My parents fought both verbally and physically in my presence, and I saw many things a little child should never see and heard words a little child should never hear. As a child I remember going to bed, pulling the covers up tightly under my chin, and praying that I could hurry up and go to sleep to shut out the noise of my parents yelling and fighting. During those early years, I had a pink musical jewelry box. Many nights I slipped out of bed, turned the key in the back of the box, and opened the lid to hear the beautiful music in hopes it would drown out the fighting in the next room. I pretended that I was the ballerina who popped up when the lid was opened and tried to let the music take me to a peaceful, magical place.

On several occasions, I awoke to broken furniture, my mother's black eye, and a weeping father making promises that it would never happen again.

As a little girl, even though I was very cute, I never felt pretty or acceptable. I longed to be cherished or valued, but I felt I was always in the way and a poor excuse for a daughter. I surmised that I was not pretty enough, smart enough, talented enough, or good enough to be the apple of anyone's eye. My parents loved me, but they were wrapped up in their own struggles and didn't always know how to show it.

When I was six years old, I skipped off to school with a new box of crayons, a swiss polka-dot dress, and fresh hope that I would be accepted. But first grade only confirmed my fears. I wasn't "enough."

From the time my first grade teacher held up the first spelling flash card, I knew I was in trouble. Back in the '60s, kindergarten was optional, and while I had attended a church-sponsored kindergarten, we focused on coloring, playing, and napping. But first grade was a whole new ball game with letters, numbers, and tests.

I remember one spelling exercise that makes my palms clammy even today. We lined our miniature wooden chairs up in a row like a choo-choo train. The teacher held up a spelling flash card for us to identify the word. If we missed the word, we had to go to the caboose. I spent most of the first grade in the caboose. For some reason, I especially had trouble with the word "the."

My brother, who proved to be very smart, had had the same teacher five years earlier, and I guess she thought that somewhere in the gene pool lurked a glimmer of hope.

I'll help her, my teacher must have thought.

So she made me a name tag that said "the" and I had to wear it for two weeks. Students came up to me and asked, "Why are you wearing that tag?" "Is your name 'the'?" "You must be stupid." "What's wrong with you?"

Well, I learned how to spell the word "the," but that's not all I learned. I learned that I was stupid, not as smart as everybody else, and once again…not enough. Mrs. Wieman

Inferiority, insecurity, and inadequacy became a filter that formed over my mind. And every thought I had, every interpretation of my little world, had to go through that sieve of deficiency. By the time I was a teenager, that filter was cemented firmly in place.

But God didn't leave me that way. Don't you just love the words "but God"? They are my two favorite words in the Bible. But God didn't leave me that way.

When I was 12 years old, I became friends with a girl in my

neighborhood, Wanda Henderson. We had known each other since first grade but truly bonded by the sixth. Wanda's mother took me under her wing and loved me as though I were her own child. Mrs. Henderson knew what was going on in my home, and she knew about my wounded heart. I loved being at the Hendersons' home. Mr. and Mrs. Henderson hugged and kissed each other in front of us and even had pet names for each other. I had never seen married people act like that before, and I watched in amazement. I didn't know why that family was so different from mine, but I knew that difference had something to do with Jesus Christ. Their home was a balm—an emotional spa.

Mrs. Henderson walked around their home doing housework and singing praise songs to the Lord. She even talked about Jesus Christ as though she knew Him personally. I thought that was strange.

Eventually, the Hendersons invited me to go to church with them, and I realized that most of the people in her church talked about Jesus Christ as though they knew Him personally. Amazingly, my family, with all of its struggles, went to church on Sundays. Yes, with all the alcohol and fighting, we went to a very politically correct, socially prestigious church—fighting all the way to the front door. We heard ear-tickling, nonoffensive sermons that were moral enough to make us feel we'd done our American duty, but not spiritual enough to convict or transform us in any way.

But the Hendersons' church was different. They talked about having a personal relationship with Jesus Christ, something I had never heard before. I wanted what they had. I went to this church and drank in every word the pastor and teachers had to say about a Savior who loved me so much He gave His life for me on Calvary's cross so that I could have eternal life. He paid the penalty for my sin. He loved me, not because I was pretty or because I could do things well, but just because I was His.

The following year, Mrs. Henderson started a Bible study for teenagers in the neighborhood, and I began a love affair with God's Word. One night, when I was 14, Mrs. Henderson sat me down on the couch.

"Sharon," she asked, "are you ready to accept Jesus as your personal Savior and Lord?"

With tears streaming down my cheeks, I answered yes.

At the very moment I accepted Christ, my spiritual transformation was complete—I went from death to life in the blink of an eye—in the time it took for me to say, "I believe." However, the transformation of my soul (mind, will, and emotions) had just begun.

At first my parents were leery of my "newfound religion," but my love for the Lord was hard to resist or deny. Two years after I gave my life to Jesus, my mother accepted Him as her personal Savior. Then three years later, through a series of events, twists, and turns that only our heavenly Father could orchestrate, my earthly father gave his life to Christ. In a matter of six years, God had worked an incredible miracle in my life and my family's lives.

But let's go back to that 14-year-old girl who was consumed with feelings of inferiority, insecurity, and inadequacy. Did those feelings melt away the moment I accepted Christ? Did they evaporate when I said the words "I believe"? Oh, dear friend, I wish I could tell you they did, but they did not. As a matter of fact, I didn't even know they were there.

Through the years I learned to compensate for my insecurities. If you had seen me as a teenager—seen my achievements and accomplishments—you would have never known I felt that way about myself or was in that type of bondage.

From the time I was 14 until I was in my early thirties, I always felt as though something was wrong with me spiritually—as though I had walked into a movie 20 minutes late and had to spend the entire time trying to figure out what was going on. I wondered why I struggled so to live the victorious Christian life. I had a wonderful husband, an amazing son, and a happy home life. I taught Bible studies at a scripturally solid church, and I surrounded myself with strong Christian friends. But something was missing—I didn't know who I was. I did not understand the change that happened in me the moment I became a Christian. I didn't understand my true identity as a child of God.

Once again, God didn't leave me that way. Something happened in my thirties. Like popcorn heating up and exploding into fluffy white clouds, certain verses of the Bible began to jump out at me: "You are chosen, and dearly loved." "You are holy." "You are a saint." I began to understand that how I saw me and how God saw me were very different. Yes, I had a spiritual makeover the moment I accepted Christ. My dead spirit became alive with Christ...born again, as Jesus told Nicodemus (John 3). But the ultimate makeover, the process of being transformed into the image of Christ, had just begun.

True Beauty

Our culture is enthralled with the idea of beauty and eternal youth, but what is true beauty? One cosmetic company made an important discovery.

A successful beauty product company asked the people in a large city to send pictures along with brief letters about the most beautiful women they knew. Within a few weeks thousands of letters were delivered to the company.

One letter in particular caught the attention of the employees, and soon it was handed to the company president. The letter was written by a young boy who was from a broken home and living in a run-down neighborhood. With spelling corrections, an excerpt from his letter said: "This beautiful woman lives down the street from me. I visit her every day. She makes me feel like the most important kid in the world. We play checkers and she listens to my problems. She understands me, and when I leave she always yells out the door that she's proud of me."

The boy ended his letter saying, "This picture shows you that she is the most beautiful woman. I hope I have a wife as pretty as her."

Intrigued by the letter, the president asked to see this woman's picture. His secretary handed him a photograph of a smiling, toothless woman, well advanced in years, sitting in a wheelchair. Sparse gray hair was pulled back in a bun. Wrinkles that formed deep furrows on her face were somehow diminished by the twinkle in her eyes.

"We can't use this woman," explained the president, smiling.

"She would show the world that our products aren't necessary to be beautiful."[1]

The little boy had discovered a valuable truth. Beauty—true beauty—begins on the inside and works its way out.

A Little Girl's Dream

I remember as a little girl sneaking into my mother's closet and slipping my child-size feet into her size seven high heels. I'd also stand on my tiptoes on a chair, pull a hat off the top shelf, and plop it on my head like an oversized lamp shade. Her satin evening jacket with sleeves that hung eight inches below my fingertips gave a nice elegant touch to my outfit. A lady going to a party would never be caught without "putting on her face," so I crept into the bathroom, opened the forbidden drawer, and created a clownish work of art on the canvas of my face. Red rouge circles on my cheeks, heaps of blue eye shadow on my munchkin lids, and smeared orange lipstick far exceeding the proper borders were finished off with a dusting of facial powder with an oversized brush.

From the time a little girl stretches on her tiptoes to get a peek in the mirror, she desires to be beautiful—perhaps just like her mommy. As the girl moves into the teen years, she experiments with makeup, delves into fashion, and attempts various hairstyles. Then it's on to makeover ideas in magazines and on talk shows. If one idea doesn't work—well, there's always next month!

Americans spend more than seven billion dollars a year on cosmetics. Magazine racks bulge each month with periodicals promising dramatic makeovers for women of every shape, color, and size. They tell us how to thin thighs, firm flab, tuck tummies, build biceps, tighten tushes, and lengthen lashes. We can learn the proper way to apply makeup, choose the best hairstyles to frame and flatter facial shapes, and determine what color wardrobe is best for our particular skin tone.

The obsession isn't limited to older women fighting the effects of aging and gravity who have expendable income. In the year 2000, American youths spent $155 billion on beauty products and trips to salons and spas—financed by willing parents.[2]

Talk show hosts' most popular programs have been those with beauty makeover themes. Viewers love to watch an artist transform a frumpy middle-aged housewife into a sophisticated cosmopolitan with just a snip of the scissors, a stroke of blush, and an updated wardrobe. Silently we wonder, *Could they do that to me?*

I'm not saying I've never read the makeover articles in the magazines or tried a few of their suggestions, and I've definitely contributed to the rising expenditure for cosmetics. But I do know this—no amount of skin creams, makeup, designer clothes, or exercise regimens will make a woman feel truly beautiful, content, or fulfilled. If we're banking on outward appearance to make us happy, we're headed for emotional bankruptcy.

Cheap Nails

One of the greatest philosophers of all time is Charlie Brown, the little round-headed kid in Charles Schulz's *Peanuts* cartoon. But even Charlie Brown has his problems. One day he was visiting his psychiatrist, Lucy. Lucy is sitting pensively behind her makeshift booth, which resembles a lemonade stand. Her shingle reads, *Psychiatric Help 5¢.*

> Frame one: Lucy says to Charlie Brown, "Your life is like a house…"
>
> Frame two: "You want your house to have a solid foundation, don't you?"
>
> Frame three: "Of course you do…"
>
> Frame four: "So don't build your house on the sand, Charlie Brown…"
>
> Frame five: A strong wind blows, knocking Lucy off her chair and the booth into a heap on the ground.
>
> Frame six: "or use cheap nails."

I see many women today who have started building their spiritual houses on the solid rock of Jesus Christ, but then they proceed to build on that foundation with the cheap nails of outward appearance, performance, possessions, power, and the praises of others. Alas, when the strong winds of adversity begin to blow, just like Lucy's makeshift psychiatric booth, we fall apart.

In 1 Corinthians 3:10-15, Paul talks about two types of building materials. One type was wood, hay, and stubble. These are what man produces. He plants and he reaps. These materials are temporary and can be burned up or lost in a moment. The other type of building material is gold, silver, and precious stones. These are what God has created, but we have to discover them—sometimes digging through mountains of dirt.

The culture's makeover ideas are temporary...wood, hay, and stubble. But the principles found in God's Word are eternal with everlasting results. We can try the beauty tips in the magazines, but true beauty occurs when we sit in God's spa and let Him perform a miracle.

Women love the idea of a day at the spa. After all, Queen Esther in the Bible stayed in a spa for an entire year before she claimed her title of Mrs. Xerxes. Her beauty regimen included six months with oils of myrrh and six months with perfumes and cosmetics (Esther 2:12). Not only that, she was assigned seven maids to take care of her every need. Now that sounds like a spa package worth looking into!

Let's face it. Women want to be beautiful. However, many fail to realize that beauty begins on the inside and works its way out. The little boy mentioned earlier discovered that beauty shines through eyes of love.

But how do you become spiritually beautiful? You will not discover the secret in magazines, talk shows, or reality TV. Inner beauty is the result of God's transforming power in the heart of a willing soul. He doesn't simply cover up our flaws; He miraculously starts from scratch and makes us new. "Therefore, if anyone is in Christ, [she] is a new creation; the old is gone, the new has come!" (2 Corinthians 5:17).

Join me now at God's spa for the ultimate beauty treatment. Your appointment has been made. God is waiting. Let's get started!

The Great Cover-Up

Getting to the Root
of the Problem

Several years ago I owned a car that continually overheated. The first time I saw the little red needle pointing to the big H on the dashboard, I assumed it meant the car was hot. It was the middle of August and, frankly, I was hot too, so I wasn't terribly alarmed. I decided to mosey on down to the dealership about 12 miles away to have it checked out. Big mistake.

After about a minute or so, steam began billowing from under the hood, the engine began knocking angrily, and the little engine that could decided it couldn't any longer. It died in the middle of a busy intersection on a Friday afternoon in five o'clock traffic. The car was towed to the dealership, where the mechanic delivered the unfortunate news.

"Mrs. Jaynes, do you see that needle that is pointing to the H?" the repairman asked. "That means the engine is runnin' hot. When you see that, you've got to stop right away. Since you kept goin,' you burned up your engine. It's a goner. You'll have to get a new one."

"That sounds expensive," I moaned.

"It'll be about four thousand dollars," he answered, while continuing to poke around under the hood.

Four thousand dollars! And all because I didn't stop the car when it overheated...all because I didn't heed the warning signs. It was a painful and costly lesson.

The mechanic installed a new engine, and you can imagine my

alarm when I noticed that little red needle pointing to H a few weeks later. This time I stopped right away. Once again, my car was towed to the dealership. Once again, they made adjustments, gave reassurances, and sent me on my way.

Over the following weeks, my car overheated three times. Each time, it was towed to the shop and the mechanic made adjustments. Finally, I said, "No more." I got rid of the car.

The trouble was, the mechanic never fixed the cause of the problem; he only tinkered with the symptoms. He fixed first one thing and then another but never got to the root of the problem to find out why the car was overheating in the first place.

How like us. We continue to tinker, fixing one flaw and then another but never getting to the root of the problem. Many times when reading the Bible, we want the "how tos" without the "why fors." In this age of instant messaging, fax machines, and microwave cooking, we want a quick fix without understanding the deep truths of Scripture. We say, "Just tell me what to do, and I'll do it." "Give me a ten-step program, and I'll check off the steps one by one." But in order to experience the ultimate beauty treatment, we must begin with ultimate truth.

Before we begin this journey, let's go back and do a little genetic research to find out why we need beautifying in the first place. Doctors require patients to fill out a questionnaire called a "health history" because the medical field has determined that certain illnesses have genetic tendencies. If your grandmother had diabetes, then you are more at risk for the same disease. If your father had heart disease, you are more likely to have it as well.

To experience the ultimate makeover, we must also look back at our parentage; however, I believe that if we want to get to the root of the problem, we must go back further than a few generations. We've got to go all the way back to the Garden—to the beginning of time.

The Real Problem

A preacher once said, "Your problem is that you don't know what the problem is. You think your problem is your problem, but that's not the problem at all. Your problem is not your problem, and that's your main problem." To determine the real problem, we need to go back to the Garden of Eden.

"In the beginning God created the heavens and the earth" (Genesis 1:1). I never tire of reading those first words in the Bible and imagining the birth of the universe and all it contains. Just think. Before the creation of the world, there was…nothing. Try thinking of nothing. We can't even do it, for to think of nothing is to think of something.

On the first day God spoke and light appeared out of the darkness. Then He drew the boundary lines to separate water on earth from the water in heaven. He gathered the water together to form the sea and called for dry ground to appear. God caused seed of every kind to appear in the soil, released flocks of birds into the sky, swarms of insects into the air, and schools of fish into the sea. On the fifth day, God created all living creatures that move along the ground.

But something was missing. God wanted something more. On the sixth day, God said, "Let Us make man in Our image" (Genesis 1:26 NASB). Then "the LORD God formed the man from the dust of the ground and breathed into his nostrils the breath of life and man became a living being" (Genesis 2:7). The word "formed" is the same word used when a potter forms a vessel with clay. What a beautiful picture as we see God lovingly shaping and molding Adam's most intricate parts with His fingertips and breathing the very breath of God into his lungs.

After each day of creation, as the sun set over the horizon, God looked at His handiwork and said, "It is good." The one exception was when He said, "It is *not good* for the man to be alone" (Genesis 2:18).

> For Adam no suitable helper was found. So the LORD God caused the man to fall into a deep sleep; and while he was sleeping, he took one of the man's ribs and closed up the

place with flesh. Then the LORD God made a woman from the rib he had taken out of the man, and he brought her to the man (Genesis 2:20-22).

The New American Standard Bible says God "fashioned" Eve. He took extra special care when He created her. Woman was God's grand finale.

Up to this point, Adam had been silent. However, when God presented him with the fair Eve, I imagine he said, "Whoa! Now *this* is good!" (Hence, whoa-man.) We don't know that for sure, but we do know that Adam's first recorded words debuted upon seeing Eve: "This is now bone of my bones and flesh of my flesh; she shall be called 'woman,' for she was taken out of man" (Genesis 2:23).

All was well in the Garden—for a while.

Three Parts of Man

I recall my kindergarten teacher saying, "Class, this year we are going to learn our ABC's and 123's." Everything else I learned over the next 16 years of formal education was built on that foundation. In order to truly experience the ultimate makeover, let's go back and review some of the basic 123's of our created being upon which we will build. As we've already discovered, you can't solve a problem if you don't understand what the real problem is.

The Bible explains God as a triune Being: God the Father, God the Son, and God the Holy Spirit. All three were present at creation. God said, "Let *Us* make man in *Our* image" (Genesis 1:26 NASB). When He created Adam and Eve in His image, He created them in three parts as well: body, soul, and spirit (1 Thessalonians 5:23).

In order to visualize the three parts of man,* let's think about the three parts of an apple. The peeling represents the body, the pulp represents the soul, and the seeds represent the spirit. The body (peeling) is the part we see. It is temporary and only exists on earth for a short period of time. Paul refers to our body as a "tent" or a temporary dwelling (2 Corinthians 5:1-4). Some refer to our body as an "earth suit." It is the vehicle through which a soul interacts

---

* For the rest of this book, when I use the word "man," I am referring to "mankind," meaning both male and female.

with the environment and other people. The body encompasses our five senses: sight, touch, taste, smell, and hearing. The body is not the man, because man can exist apart from his earthly body (2 Corinthians 12:2-3). As one inexperienced preacher said while standing by the casket at his first funeral, "What we have here is an empty shell. The nut has already left us!"

We also have a soul. The soul houses the mind, will, and emotions. It allows us to think, choose, and feel emotions. The brain is part of the body, but the mind is part of the soul. The mind uses the brain to function, much like software uses a computer to run. The soul determines personality. Some commentators note that we are only two parts: immaterial and material, or body and spirit/soul. However, others believe we are in three parts: body, soul, and spirit. I believe we are three. The writer of Hebrews notes, "The word of God is living and active. Sharper than any double-edged sword, it penetrates even to dividing soul and spirit, joints and marrow; it judges the thoughts and attitudes of the heart" (Hebrews 4:12).

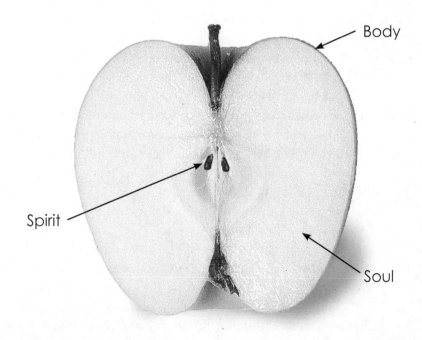

Body

Spirit

Soul

There is nothing worse than purchasing a beautiful, highly polished Red Delicious apple and biting into it, only to find it mealy and mushy on the inside. Well, maybe there is something worse—a physically beautiful woman who is rotten to the core. Solomon says that's like putting a "gold ring in a pig's snout" (Proverbs 11:22). What a waste.

Becky experienced this firsthand when she was 19 years old. She was performing as a runway model at her hometown department store. She was 5'2" and 100 pounds, just the perfect size to model apparel from the petite department. But she had always longed to be tall and slender like the runway models from the big cities. On one occasion, the management of the store where Becky worked flew in a New York model to add to the excitement of a fashion show event. Becky was thrilled to watch as a professional paraded up and down the runway with poise and elegance.

Becky explained, "I can remember standing behind a rack of clothes and peering admiringly as the 5'8" sleek blonde glided up and down the runway with the grace and poise of a queen. 'Oh, God,' I prayed, 'how I wish I could be like her.'"

After the fashion show was over, Becky was gathering her belongings from backstage when she overheard the model in a fit of rage.

"I don't even know what happened," Becky said. "All I know is that this beautiful woman, whom I had so admired, almost worshipped, was spewing the filthiest language I had ever heard and slinging clothes and shoes all around the room. I ran out of the store and cried all the way home. Disappointment and disillusionment filled my heart. 'Oh, God,' I prayed once again, 'please don't ever let me be like her.'"

Becky had learned a valuable lesson about true beauty. "Often behind silken apparel lies a threadbare soul."[1]

The core of man is the spirit. While the body is temporal, the spirit is eternal. "We are confident, yes, well pleased rather to be absent from the body and to be present with the Lord" (2 Corinthians 5:8 NKJV). Paul knew when his body died, his spirit would live in heaven with God. Just as the body is necessary for people to relate to one another, the spirit is necessary for man to relate to God.

In the apple model, the seeds in the core represent the spirit. Just as the seeds determine the type of apple (Granny Smith, Red Delicious, Rome) the spirit determines a person's true identity. The Bible states that there are two types of "seed" that determine if you are a bad apple or a good apple. One is perishable and the other is imperishable. "You have been born again, not of perishable seed, but of imperishable, through the living and enduring word of God" (1 Peter 1:23). We will take a look at the two different types in just a moment.

At creation, Adam and Eve were created in the image of God and perfect in every way. Their bodies had no genetic defects or flaws, their souls were naked and unashamed, and their spirits were in perfect union with God—two prize apples!

Three Aspects of Life

Man was created in three parts, and he was alive in every area. "The LORD God formed the man from the dust of the ground and breathed into his nostrils the breath of life, and the man became a living being" (Genesis 2:7). The best description of the word "life" is found in the Greek forms of the word. We have one word for "love" and the Greeks had three: *agape* (unconditional Christlike love), *phileo* (brotherly love), and *eros* (sexual love). Likewise, we have one word for "life" and the Greeks had three: *bios, psyche,* and *zoe.*

1. *Bios* is the life of the body. (This is where we get the word "biosphere.")

2. *Psyche* is the life of the soul: mind, will, and emotions. (This is where we get the word "psychology.")

3. *Zoe* is the life of the spirit.

Adam and Eve were fully alive in all three dimensions. Their bodies, souls, and spirits were in complete communion with God.

Three Glowing Attributes

Adam and Eve had no needs. Instead of needs, they had three glowing attributes.

1. Significance: Adam and Eve had great significance as rulers of all the creatures in the entire earth. They had a job to do.

2. Safety and security: Adam and Eve were very secure in their relationship with God. All their needs were cared for.

3. Sense of belonging: Adam and Eve were in perfect union and communion with God and each other. They lived in community.

Three Temptations

Adam and Eve had a wonderfully fulfilling life. They lived in God's presence. He walked and talked with them in the cool of the evening, and He met all of their needs.

> I give you every seed-bearing plant on the face of the whole earth and every tree that has fruit with seed in it. They will be yours for food. And to all the beasts of the earth and all the birds of the air and all the creatures that move on the ground—everything that has the breath of life in it—I give every green plant for food (Genesis 1:29).

God placed only one restriction on the pair. "You are free to eat from any tree in the garden, but you must not eat from the tree of the knowledge of good and evil, for when you eat of it you will surely die" (Genesis 2:16-17).

In Genesis 3, we see where our ancestors made a grave decision that affected every person born thereafter. Satan came to Eve in the form of a serpent and tempted her with the one restriction placed on her by God. How did he do it?

1. He questioned God. "Did God really say, 'You must not eat from any tree in the garden'?" (Genesis 3:1).

2. He denied God. " 'You will not surely die,' the serpent said
   to the woman" (verse 4).

3. He caused her to doubt God's justice. "For God knows that
   when you eat of it your eyes will be opened, and you will
   be like God, knowing good and evil" (verse 5).

Satan is the great deceiver who takes what worked in the Garden
and continues to use the same tactics today. He is not very creative,
but he is highly effective. It is important to understand his tactics in
order to recognize and defeat them. Paul said he was not ignorant
of the devil's schemes (2 Corinthians 2:11 NASB), and we shouldn't
be, either. Satan tempts us to question God. *Has God said you must
stay married to a man who doesn't meet your needs?* He tempts us to
deny God. *God wouldn't count it as a sin for you to seek happiness
elsewhere.* He tempts us to doubt God's justice. *What kind of God
is He who would deny you the right to find happiness in the arms of a
different man who appreciates you?*

The basis for Eve's temptation, and for ours as well, is the lie that
God is somehow holding out on us. Think about it. Can you think
of any temptation that does not have its root in that lie? Eve had it
all! And yet Satan came to her and whispered, "God is holding out
on you. There's more to be had than your perfect world. You can be
like God. You can be in control."

This is Satan's strategic battle plan, and his desire is to catch us
off guard. Let's consider the following scenario about someone we'll
call Anna.

Anna was a beautiful woman who loved opera and the stage.
She had an incredible voice, and when she sang in church, it was
as though she was ushering the congregation right into the throne
room of God. In her single years, she had aspirations of joining an
opera company, but she put those plans on hold to settle down with
the man of her dreams. She and Rob had no children, but they were
very content and very much in love.

One night, while enjoying a romantic dinner at a restaurant with
her husband, she struck up a conversation with their waitress. It

seems she was auditioning for an opera the next day and was a bit nervous. The mention of an opera audition piqued Anna's interest and she inquired further.

"An opera?" she asked. "Which one?"

Rob knew the particular opera the waitress mentioned. It was about the tumultuous life of a prostitute. He watched as Anna grew animated with excitement about the possibility of auditioning herself. He voiced his concerns about the sordid theme of the opera, but Anna ignored his questions.

Enter Satan. I envision him whispering in her ear. "Anna, this is what you've always wanted—a chance to get back on stage again. So what if the theme is a bit off-color. It's art! God hasn't said not to do such operas. It's not in the Bible. Rob is just being overprotective. Besides, he knows you might be successful, and he's probably just jealous. Who knows? You might even be able to witness to the cast. Besides, you deserve this chance."

"Oh, Rob," Anna said. "God doesn't mind me being in this opera. It's art, and besides, maybe I will be able to witness to the cast!"

"I don't feel good about this," Rob argued. "Participating in an opera with this type of story line can't be honoring to God."

Enter Satan: "It's not going to hurt you to try out. You might not get the part anyway. Besides, Rob's being controlling. Aren't you your own woman? Are you going to let a man tell you what you can and can't do?"

"Rob, it's not a big deal," Anna countered. "I might not get the part anyway. Besides, you're being controlling. I'm strong enough to handle this."

"Even so," Rob answered, "just know that I do not want you to do this."

The romantic dinner was over.

Two weeks later, Anna auditioned for the opera and secured the female lead—that of a prostitute. Satan had slithered his way into the cracked door and gained a foothold. Anna sang more passionately than ever before, flaunted her risqué dressed body across the stage, and enjoyed the kisses of her leading man. Rob watched helplessly as his wife became another woman before his very eyes, both on and off stage.

Three weeks after the close of the opera, while Rob was gone to the grocery store, Anna packed up her belongings and left, never to return. It seems her leading man led her right off the stage and into his arms.

Satan grinned and made another check mark on his victory board.

Dear sister, do not be deceived. Satan is a liar and the father of lies (John 8:44). He still tells lies today. He still deceives those who will listen in the same way he deceived Eve. He tempted her in the three areas of her being, and he tempts us there as well.

"When the woman saw that the tree was

1. "good for food,"—her body

2. "and that it was a delight to the eyes,"—her soul: mind, will, and emotions

3. "and that the tree was desirable to make one wise,"—her spirit (she believed the lie that if she ate from this tree, she would be like God)

"she took from its fruit and ate; and she gave also to her husband with her, and he ate. Then the eyes of both of them were opened, and they knew that they were naked; and they sewed fig leaves together and made themselves loin coverings" (Genesis 3:6-7 NASB). At that moment shame entered the world, and their relationship with God was broken. They were banished from God's presence and cast out of the Garden with cherubim waving flaming swords to prevent them from entering again (Genesis 3:23-24).

The Penalty

Do you remember God's penalty for eating from the tree of the knowledge of good and evil? The punishment was death. But did they die? This is where so many have missed a vital truth. *Yes, they did die.* Their bodies did not die right away, even though the process was set into motion. However, at that very moment of disobedience, their spirits died. Their *zoe* life was taken away, and every person who has been born since that time has been born with a live body, but a dead spirit. "Therefore, just as sin entered the world through one man, and death through sin, and in this way death came to all men, because all sinned" (Romans 5:12; see also Ephesians 2:1; 1 Corinthians 15:21-22). While most think the penalty was being cast out of the Garden, the real penalty was spiritual death.

Think back to the apple model for a moment. If the seed of an apple were to go bad, the entire apple would suffer as well. Adam and Eve's "seed," or spirit, died, and they became rotten to the core. But God didn't leave His most precious creation—man—that way. In *The Gift to All People,* Max Lucado gives the hope of the promise in the Garden: "The moment the forbidden fruit touched the lips of Eve, the shadow of the cross appeared on the horizon. And between that moment and the moment the man with the mallet placed the spike against the wrist of God, a master plan was fulfilled."

One night, a Pharisee named Nicodemus came to Jesus and wanted to know more about His teachings. Jesus told him, "I tell you the truth, no one can see the kingdom of God unless he is born again" (John 3:3).

Nicodemus was confused and asked, "Surely he cannot enter a second time into his mother's womb to be born!" (verse 4).

"Jesus answered, 'I tell you the truth, no one can enter the kingdom of God unless he is born of water and the Spirit. Flesh gives birth to flesh, but the Spirit gives birth to spirit. You should not be surprised at my saying, "You must be born again." The wind blows where it pleases. You hear its sound, but you cannot tell where it comes from or where it is going. So it is with everyone born of the Spirit'" (John 3:5-8).

Jesus explained to Nicodemus that in order for a person to enter heaven, he or she must have a new birth of the spirit. Why? Because our spirit, our *zoe* life, died when Adam and Eve chose to disobey and we must be *spiritually* born again.

Christ is not interested in religious people with dead spirits. He's interested in alive spirits who worship Him in spirit and in truth (John 4:23).

The Three Glaring Needs

Before the fall, Eve had no needs. She felt significant, safe, and secure, and she had a sense of belonging. She was perfect and complete, lacking nothing. However, after she disobeyed God, her *zoe* life was taken away and her glowing attributes became glaring needs:

1. Eve lost her sense of significance and felt shame.

2. Eve lost her sense of safety and security and felt fear.

3. Eve lost her sense of belonging and felt emptiness and rejection.

She tried wearing a new outfit, but that didn't cover her feelings of insecurity. She tried hiding so no one would notice her imperfections, but she forgot that God sees everything. She even tried having a couple of kids to fill the emptiness and restore her sense of belonging, but their failures only accentuated her inadequacies. No matter what she tried to fill the void, Eve's glaring needs were blinding. She was ugly from the inside out and rotten to the core.

And this brings us to the real problem—the reason we need transformation. Our glaring needs mask the beauty that God intended for each and every one of His children. God desires for us to turn to Him and allow those needs to be met in Jesus Christ alone. Satan desires for us to attempt to get those needs met in our own way and by our own strength through people, things, and circumstances. Our dead spirit and sinful nature causes darkness and ugliness to rule in our minds, wills, and emotions, but Jesus can remove the darkness and fill us with His light. He is the beautifier. The door is always open, He is always available, and the price has already been paid.

Gin was a woman who experienced the makeover power of Jesus Christ. She came to America from Korea in search of a better, more prosperous life. In order to adjust as quickly as possible to the new culture, she registered for an English language class at the local air force base. A corporal who taught the class became enamored of this beautiful petite china doll from Korea. After a few months, they fell in love and were married.

Gin's new husband took her to a church service one Sunday, and for the first time she heard the story of creation, the fall of man, the resulting sin nature of all mankind, and the redemptive power of Jesus Christ to save us and make us new.

She went home that evening and looked in the mirror. Gin was horrified at what she saw.

In halting English, Gin explained. "When I looked in the mirror, I looked ugly. My face was dark and dirty. I could see sin. I had never noticed before, but the sin made me ugly."

The next week, Gin went back to church. When the pastor invited listeners to accept Jesus Christ as Lord and Savior at the close of the service, Gin ran forward. With tears in her eyes she fell on her knees and made the most important transforming decision in her life.

"After I accepted Christ, I went back home and looked in the mirror again. Now I was beautiful. The sin and darkness were gone and my face was shining!"

The Potemkin Village

Purportedly there was a time in 1787 when the empress Catherine II made a visit to a recent conquest—the Russian Crimea. In order to impress the empress, Russian minister Potemkin erected fake villages along the desolate banks of the Dnieper River. Facades of settlements were erected far enough away from the riverbank so that the monarch and her traveling party could not tell that they were only facades as they sailed by. The glowing village fires were meant to comfort the monarch and her entourage as they surveyed the land, but the reality was her conquest was a barren impoverished wasteland.

How like today's obsession with appearance. We put on facades of a happy home with 2.5 kids, laughing singles at a darkened bar, satisfied executives in power suits, or perfectly sculpted bodies at the gym—mere Potemkin villages. Just like Adam and Eve in the Garden, men and women still attempt the great cover-up. But when the King of the universe passes by, He sees past the facade. Like a cameraman who pulls his camera back away from the set, God sees what is real. He doesn't want us to live in Potemkin villages, putting up a facade. He desires to transform us and conform us into the image of Christ. He longs for us to be forever new.

When Gin had her spiritual makeover, she became a new creation in Christ (2 Corinthians 5:17). God has issued a gift certificate for each and every one of us to experience an ultimate beauty treatment in the spa of His love. All we have to do is accept His invitation. What are we waiting for?

A Brand-New You

Exchanging the Old for the New

Julianna came out of the womb ready to meet every challenge with determination, every celebration with enthusiasm, and every mystery with the passion of discovery. Her fiery red hair matched her fiery personality. She never did anything halfway, but with the throttle full speed ahead. Of the Prices' three children, Julianna was the one who frequented the emergency room for stitches due to throwing caution to the wind as she whirled through her childhood.

One day when Julianna was 12 years old, she rushed out her front door on her way to dance class. She slammed the door behind her as she hurried to catch her ride, but the door closed before all of her fingers followed her body across the threshold. Now you have probably have slammed your fingers in a door a time or two, and can remember wincing a bit. But Julianna never does anything halfway. She jerked to a sudden halt, spun around quickly, and saw her appendages trapped in the closed door. When she opened the door to remove her hand, she was horrified to discover that all of it was not there. She had amputated the upper third of her second right finger.

"Help! Somebody help me! I've just cut off my finger!"

Fortunately, the woman picking her up for dance class was a nurse. She rushed to the screaming ballerina. "Julianna, where's your mom?" she asked.

She's not here," Julianna answered between sobs. "Nobody's here but Daniel."

"Quick," the neighbor instructed. "Let's put some pressure on that nub. Daniel, come help us!"

Daniel, Julianna's 15-year-old brother, ran down the stairs at the cry for help.

"Julianna's just cut her finger off. You have to find it. We've got to put it in ice and take her to the hospital right away."

A pale-faced Daniel went to the scene of the accident. As he hung his head, he saw the finger lying at his feet. Trying not to lose his breakfast, Daniel picked up his sister's digit in a towel and handed it over to the nurse.

Well, the good news is that they got to the hospital in time. The skilled doctor put Humpty Dumpty back together again and told them to pray that the finger would reattach.

"We'll keep our fingers crossed," he said with a grin as he walked out of the treatment room.

A few days later Julianna unwrapped the bandages, afraid of what she might find underneath. What she saw was not a pretty sight. Instead of a finger, she saw a black mushroomlike thimble sitting atop her nub.

"Doctor, we took the bandage off today. It's black and crusty and looks like a mushroom cap," her mom reported. "It looks dead."

"That's fine," he reassured her. "Don't worry. If nature is working properly, and it sounds like it is, the top will turn black, but underneath, nerves and blood vessels are reattaching. Underneath the thimble, a new finger is forming. She needs the old part in order for the new part to form underneath. In about three weeks, we'll know if the procedure worked. Just keep it wrapped and clean."

A few weeks after the accident, Julianna came to spend the night with us while she was attending a dance camp in my hometown. I had the pleasure of her company and the displeasure of changing her bandage. Her description was accurate.

Four weeks after Julianna had returned home, she wrote me a thank-you note for having her in our home. She ended by saying, "P.S. Guess what? My crusty thimble fell off and I have a new finger!"

Now, don't ask me how this happened. It's a mystery to me. But Scripture tells of another mystery that is just as amazing. Another grafting process that is just as miraculous. As we have already seen, when God warned Adam and Eve not to eat of the fruit of the tree of knowledge of good and evil, He warned them that their punishment for disobedience would be death. They did eat—and immediately their spirits died. Their *zoe* life was taken away and they were cut off from God. As a result, every person after that time has been born with a dead spirit, including you and me.

But God didn't leave us that way. God demonstrated His love toward us, that while we were still sinners (cut off, dead, rotten to the core), Christ died for us and made it possible for us to be grafted onto the living root—Himself (Romans 5:8; 11:17-18). At the very moment we accept Jesus Christ as our Savior, we receive a new living spirit (*zoe* life) to replace our old dead spirit. God performs a spiritual transformation in the twinkling of an eye—in the time it takes for us to say, "I believe." However, God's process of shaping and molding us into the image of Christ takes a lifetime.

Let's take a look at what happens during our spiritual transformation.

The Path to Zoe Life

Makeover articles in magazines show before and after pictures to get the full effect. Sometimes the transformation is so dramatic we wonder, "Is that really the same person?" Likewise, after we meet Jesus Christ, our change should be so dramatic that our friends and family members wonder if *we* are the same person. Here's the good news—we're not!

Let's take a look at what our "before Christ" picture looks like. Just as it is important to know who you are in Christ, it is important to know who you were without Him. Many of the Scriptures that follow may be familiar to you. If so, don't gloss over them quickly, but read them slowly and carefully, as if you are seeing them for the first time.

Before knowing Christ:

- We were dead in our transgressions and sin (Ephesians 2:1).

- We gratified the craving of our sinful nature and followed its desires and thoughts (Ephesians 2:3).

- We were separated from Christ and without hope (Ephesians 2:12).

- We were far away from God (Ephesians 2:13).

- We were foreigners and aliens (Ephesians 2:19).

- We were enemies of God (Colossians 1:21).

- We were in darkness (1 Thessalonians 5:4).

- We were darkness (Ephesians 5:8).

- We were slaves of sin (Romans 6:17).

- We were unable to please God (Romans 8:8).

Not a very pretty picture. Oh, we may look good on the outside, and our peeling may look shiny, polished, and desirable, but before we know Christ, we are ugly on the inside and rotten to the core. We can try to cover up the ugliness with modern day fig leaves, such as financial success, flashy cars, impeccable makeup, coordinating accessories, or name brand clothes, but what lies beneath is still dead. Our attempts are akin to putting makeup on a corpse. You can't hide what lies beneath.

Forever New

Sometimes it is easy to read about Adam and Eve's failure in the Garden and think to ourselves, *How could they be so disobedient?* But in reality, this is not Adam and Eve's story alone. It's our story as well. We make decisions daily that either dishonor or honor God. We disobey, take charge of our own lives, and become Lord of our own ring. Then, like Eve, we try to cover up our shame and even attempt to hide from God.

Do you know the first question God asked in the Bible? After Adam and Eve cowered in the bushes, hiding from God, He asked,

"Where are you?" God knew exactly where they were, what they had done, and how the enemy had tricked them. However, He decided to remain in relationship with them and begin the process of restoration which was completed on Calvary's cross. He asks the same question of us today as we attempt to hide... *Where are you?*

As I said earlier, I think "but God" are two of the most beautiful words in Scripture. The Bible says, "But God demonstrates His own love toward us, in that while we were yet sinners, Christ died for us" (Romans 5:8 NASB). When did we become sinners? The first time we sinned? No, we were born sinners, and that sin is what separated us from God. While we were yet sinners, He became the perfect sacrifice for us, not to cover our sin, but to cleanse us forever—once and for all. Salvation Army Officer John Allen once said, "I deserved to be damned in hell, but God interfered."[1] God interfered, intervened, and intercepted our death sentence. He sent His Son, who paid the penalty for our sin and all we have to do to receive the pardon is to accept His wonderful gift.

How do we receive the gift certificate to a spiritual makeover? "If you confess with your mouth 'Jesus as Lord,' and believe in your heart that God raised him from the dead, you will be saved" (Romans 10:9). When you accept Jesus Christ as your own personal Savior, you are freed from the penalty of sin (spiritual death and eternal separation from God), and He gives you a new living spirit. "Salvation is moving from living death to deathless life."[2]

"All this is from God, who reconciled us [joined us back together] to himself through Christ" (2 Corinthians 5:18). Let me paint this picture in your mind. Imagine standing at the ledge of a vast canyon called Sin—a canyon so wide and deep that you cannot see the other side or the ground below. Your heart longs to somehow cross this canyon of emptiness because God resides on the other side. The only thing separating you from God is this canyon of Sin, and the passage is humanly impossible.

God longs for you to be in His presence even more than you long to be in His. He knew you could not cross on your own, so He did something amazing. God sent His only Son, Jesus, to die a cruel sacrificial death on a Roman cross. When Jesus breathed His last breath and the cross was lowered from the mound, one end now rests at your feet and the other bridges the ravine to rest on the other side.

There is a way to cross this canyon of Sin! What was humanly impossible was made supernaturally possible through the cross of Christ, and you can run across the cross into the loving arms of God who "reconciled us to himself through Christ."

Why did God do this for us? "For God so loved the world that he gave his one and only Son, that whoever believes in him shall not perish but have eternal life" (John 3:16). Remember the three Greek words for life: *bios, psyche,* and *zoe*? Guess which word for life is in John 3:16? *Zoe*—life of the spirit! When you become a Christian, your spirit is reborn and you experience a spiritual makeover at that very moment. "Therefore, if anyone is in Christ, he is a new creation; the old has gone, the new has come!" (2 Corinthians 5:17). We, along with the apostle Paul, can say, "I have been crucified with Christ and I no longer live, but Christ lives in me. The life I live in the body, I live by faith in the Son of God, who loved me and gave himself for me" (Galatians 2:20).

But what about our glaring needs? "So then as through one transgression there resulted condemnation to all men, even so through one act of righteousness, there resulted justification of life to all men" (Romans 5:18 NASB). All were condemned because of Adam's disobedience, and all who accept Jesus are freed because of His obedience. At the moment of your salvation, everything you lost when Adam and Eve sinned in the Garden was returned to you in Jesus Christ when He gave His life on the cross. Once again you have

1. Significance because of who you are in Christ.

2. Safety and security because of what you have in Christ.

3. Belonging because of where you are in Christ.

Your glaring needs have been fulfilled and transformed into your glowing attributes. The question is, why don't we act as though our needs have been fulfilled? Why do we continue to struggle with feelings of shame, fear, loneliness, and rejection? Why do we continue to try to get our needs met by our own means? Because even though our spirits are changed in an instant, our minds must be renewed, our wills must come under the control of the Holy Spirit, and our emotions must be reprogrammed.

Salvation: Past, Present, and Future

Before creation, there was no time. God created time when He made the sun and the moon. "There was evening, and there was morning—the first day" (Genesis 1:5). Then He created man and woman and placed them in the time-space continuum. For God, there is still no time. God sees everything at once. He is the same yesterday, today, and forever (Hebrews 13:8). A thousand years are like a day in His sight (2 Peter 3:8). He sees the entire span of time, from beginning to the end, all at once. But we are creatures constrained by time.

When we use the words, "I have been saved," we think of time dimensionally. Salvation for us involves the past, present, and future.

1. In the past, we were saved from the *penalty* of sin at the moment of salvation. Theologians call this *justification*. We are declared not guilty—just as though we had never sinned. Justification is not due to anything we do on our own; it is a gift of grace and mercy from God. We are not saved by how we behave but by what we believe.

2. In the present, we are being saved from the *power* of sin as we become conformed to the image of Christ. Theologians call this *sanctification*. While justification is an act, sanctification is a process. Justification is the declaration of "not guilty" by a judge *about* us while sanctification is the process of the Great Physician operating *in* us. This is our focus of ultimate makeover.

3. In the future, we will be saved from the *presence* of sin. One day we will leave this earth and join Jesus in heaven for

all eternity. There will be no more death, mourning, tears, or pain. Hallelujah, there will be no more sin (Revelation 21:1-5). This is when we will experience *glorification.*

From beginning to end, salvation is a work of God. At the same time, the Bible teaches that we have a responsibility in the continuing process of being conformed to the image of Christ. We are told: "put off your old self" (Ephesians 4:22); "[renew] your mind" (Romans 12:2); "[clothe] yourself with Christ" (Galatians 3:27); "continue to work out your salvation" (Philippians 2:12); "press on toward the goal" (Philippians 3:14). It's all about God, but He has "sovereignly chosen to allow us to participate in His work."[3]

Now that we've taken a look at the mystery of God's time line, let's examine who we are right now...today!

Your New Identity

There's a game I've played many times at conferences and retreats as an icebreaker activity. Each person has the name of a famous or infamous person taped to her back. The women in the room walk around giving each other clues about who they "are." "You always put off worrying until tomorrow." "You had so many children you didn't know what to do." "You were the queen of soul." The point of the game is to figure out your identity. Once you guess correctly, you take a seat.

As I play that game, I am always struck with its similarity to real life. Many times we determine our identity by what others tell us about ourselves. *You are so smart. You are a loser. You are so pretty. You could do anything you set your mind to. You are so ugly. You are so fat.* After a while, those messages determine how we see ourselves, whether true or false. It is only a mature person who realizes that just because someone perceives you a certain way, it doesn't make that perception true.

One of the greatest blessings of becoming a Christian and experiencing spiritual transformation is receiving a new identity. In the Bible, when God touched and changed a person's life, He sometimes changed his or her name. He said, "You will be called by a new name that the mouth of the LORD will bestow" (Isaiah 62:2). Saul became Paul. Abram became Abraham. Sarai became Sarah. Jacob became Israel. Simon became Peter.

Likewise, when we accept Christ, God gives us a new identity and a new name. If we want to know our true identity, we need only look in the mirror of God's Word to discover it. It may be different from what you've heard others say about you, but which do you think is more accurate? Who do you think has a better perception of who you are, your Creator or other creatures just like yourself? If you are a Christian today, the following verses describe your new identity.[4]

My Identity in Christ

Matthew 5:13	I am the salt of the earth.
Matthew 5:14	I am the light of the world.
Matthew 6:26	I am valuable to God.
John 14:20	I am indwelled by Christ. His Spirit lives in me.
John 15:1,5	I am a branch of the True Vine.
John 15:15	I am Christ's friend.
John 15:16	I am chosen and appointed by Christ to go and bear fruit.
Romans 5:9	I am justified by Christ's blood.
Romans 5:10	I am reconciled to God through Christ's death and saved through Christ's life.
Romans 6:18	I am set free from sin and a slave of righteousness.
Romans 8:1	I am free from condemnation.
Romans 8:2	I am free in Christ.

Romans 8:17	I am a child of God and a co-heir with Christ.
Romans 8:37	I am more than a conqueror through Christ.
Romans 15:7	I am accepted by Christ.
1 Corinthians 2:16	I have the mind of Christ.
1 Corinthians 3:16	I am a temple of God. His Spirit lives in me.
1 Corinthians 6:11	I am washed, justified, and sanctified through Christ.
1 Corinthians 6:19	I am a temple of God.
1 Corinthians 12:27	I am part of Christ's body.
2 Corinthians 2:15	I am the fragrance of Christ.
2 Corinthians 5:17	I am a new creation.
2 Corinthians 5:20	I am an ambassador for Christ and a minister of reconciliation.
2 Corinthians 5:21	I am the righteousness of God in Christ.
Galatians 3:13	I am redeemed from the curse of the law.
Galatians 4:7	I am a child of God and an heir of God.
Ephesians 1:1	I am a saint.
Ephesians 1:3	I am blessed with every spiritual blessing in Christ.
Ephesians 1:5	I am adopted into God's family.
Ephesians 1:7	I am redeemed and forgiven through Christ's blood.

Ephesians 1:11	I am chosen by God.
Ephesians 1:13	I am sealed by God with the Holy Spirit.
Ephesians 2:5	I am now alive with Christ.
Ephesians 2:10	I am God's workmanship created in Christ Jesus to do good works which God prepared in advance for me to do.
Ephesians 2:19	I am a fellow citizen with God's people and a member of God's household.
Philippians 4:13	I am able to do all things through Christ who gives me strength.
Philippians 3:20	I am a citizen of heaven.
Colossians 1:13	I am rescued from the dominion of darkness and brought into the kingdom of the Son God loves (kingdom of light).
Colossians 1:22	I am holy in God's sight, without blemish and free of accusation.
Colossians 2:10	I am complete in Christ (NASB).
Colossians 3:12	I am chosen by God, holy and dearly loved.
Colossians 3:3	I am hidden with Christ in God.
1 Peter 2:9	I am of a chosen people, a royal priesthood, a holy nation, a people belonging to God to declare the praises of him who called me out

	of darkness into his wonderful light.
1 Peter 2:11	I am an alien and stranger to this world.
1 Peter 5:8	I am an enemy of the devil.
1 John 1:9	I am forgiven of my sins.
1 John 3:1-2	I am now a child of God.
1 John 5:18	I am born of God and the evil one (the devil) cannot harm me.
Revelation 21:9	I am the bride of Christ.

That is a lot to put on a name tag, but that is your new identity. Neil Anderson, in his book *Victory over the Darkness,* notes,

> The reason so many Christians are not enjoying the maturity and freedom which is their inheritance in Christ is because they hold wrong self-perceptions. They don't see themselves as they really are in Christ. They don't understand the dramatic change which occurred in them the moment they trusted in Him. They don't see themselves the way God sees them, and to that degree they suffer from a poor self-image. They don't grasp their true identity. They identify themselves with the wrong Adam.[5]

In that paragraph, Dr. Anderson described me perfectly. I had no idea who I was, what I had, or where I was in Christ. As God opened my eyes to the truth, I realized that how I saw me and how God saw me were in stark contrast to one another. I came to a crisis of belief...whom was I going to believe?

Remember the apple model? The seeds of an apple determine its identity as a Granny Smith, Red Delicious, or Rome. Likewise, your "seed" determines your identity. Your old seed was the same as Adam's (corruptible, disobedient, and enslaved to sin). Your new seed is the same as Christ's (pure, righteous, and holy). You are forever new, and the core of your being has been changed—your very nature transformed. "For you have been born again, not of perishable seed, but of imperishable, through the living and enduring word of God" (2 Peter 1:23).

I can hear some of you mumbling, "Well, I sure don't feel righteous and holy. I don't feel like a saint. I don't feel like a new creation." I'd say the predominant word in those statements is "feel." We must answer this question: Is the above list of Scriptures the truth? Yes, it is the truth, whether we feel like it or not.

If we continue to label ourselves as sinners rather than saints, we are saying our identity is based on our performance and not the finished work of Christ on the cross. We are basing our identity on our behavior rather than our new birth, on our performance rather than our position. I know many people with "good" behavior who are not going to heaven because of their position—they have not accepted Christ and are spiritually dead. I am not saying that once we become a Christian we no longer sin. That would be a ridiculous lie. John wrote, "If we claim to be without sin, we deceive ourselves and the truth is not in us" (1 John 1:8). I am saying that our sin no longer defines who we are. I was a sinner who was saved by grace. Now I'm a saint who sometimes sins. It is vital that we understand the difference between "having sin" and "being sin."

I saw a bumper sticker once that read "God said it. I believe it. It's true."

But actually, God said it, therefore it's true whether we believe it or not. I have to ask myself if I am going to walk through life being controlled by my emotions or being controlled by the truth. I've often heard that emotions or feelings are like the tail on a dog. I can assure you that if a dog jumps over a fence, the tail will follow. If you start walking in the truth, your emotions will follow—eventually. Someone once said, "Faith is acting like God tells the truth." It is one thing to say we believe God tells the truth, but it is quite another to act like it.

There are many people who are trying desperately to become

someone they already are in Christ. To be free, we must grasp our true identity as a child of God. There is nothing we can do to make our new identity in Christ more true or less true than it is at the moment of salvation. However, there is much we can do to make it have more power in our lives…believe.

Present-Tense Believing

In Ephesians 1:13 we read: "And you also were included in Christ when you heard the word of truth, the gospel of your salvation. Having *believed,* you were marked in him with a seal, the promised Holy Spirit." We believed—past tense—and were saved, sealed, delivered… we're His! It was completed in the past, once and for all time.

Now let's read a little further down in Ephesians 1:18. "I pray also that the eyes of your heart may be enlightened in order that you may know the hope to which he has called you, the riches of his glorious inheritance in the saints, and his incomparably great power for us who *believe.*" We received salvation when we believed (past tense). We have great power when we believe (present tense).

The Greek word for "believe" that is used in Ephesians 1:18 is a present active participle. That means it is a continuous action verb. "In other words, the promise given in verses 19-20 is not applied to those 'having believed' as in verse 13 where they had believed to become Christians. Rather, it is applied to those who are presently, actively, and yes, continually believing God."[6]

Maybe you believed in Jesus and experienced salvation. But do you believe the Word of God by faith and understand that you have the same power working in your life that raised Jesus from the dead? It is available to you…if you believe. The ultimate transformation begins with ultimate truth and continues to grow as we believe and practice walking in that truth.

A sapling planted in the ground does not become more of a tree as it grows. It just becomes stronger and more mature. "The growth stage cannot alter the organism; it can only ensure that the organism reaches its greatest potential."[7] As a tree's roots grow deeper, it produces a greater display of leaves, more shade and beauty for others to enjoy, and stronger branches for tire swings and birds' nests, but it's still a tree. There is nothing you can do to make your identity more true than at the very moment you accept Christ as your Savior, but there is much you can do to make it have more power in your life as you mature.

It begins by believing the truth. It is a step of faith. "Faith is being sure of what we hope for and certain of what we do not see" (Hebrews 11:1). It is "acting like God tells the truth."

"But I don't act like a saint," I hear you say. Sometimes I may not act like a saint, but that is my new identity nonetheless. My identity is not based on performance but position, not on how I act but who I am. When I was five years old, I acted more like a boy than a girl. I climbed trees, shunned dolls, threw rocks, and balked at having to wear a shirt. But, I can assure you, that didn't make me a boy—I was a girl.

Let me give you another example. When I was born physically, I had a father. His name was Allan Edwards. As his daughter, I have his blood coursing through my veins. There is nothing I can do to change that. What if I ran away from home and even changed my name? Would I still be an Edwards? Yes, my name may be different, but I would still be an Edwards.

There is nothing I can do to change my position as Allan Edwards' physical daughter, and once I have accepted Christ, there is nothing I can do to change my position as God's spiritual daughter. My behavior may change the closeness of the relationship with both, but my position as my earthly father's child and my heavenly Father's child, stands unchanged.

Do me a favor. Put this book down in your lap. Now clasp your hands together and notice which thumb is on top, your right thumb or left. Open your hands, shift each finger over a notch, and clasp them together again with the opposite thumb on top. Does that new position feel uncomfortable? Likewise, accepting your new identity in Christ may feel uncomfortable at first, but by spending time with the One who changed you, you'll begin to see yourself as God sees you. Absolutely beautiful!

Debbie's Acceptance of Her New Identity

Debbie's paternal grandparents had both a housekeeper and groundskeeper who lived in their basement apartment. Silas and Nina were like part of the family and had lived with the grandparents for as long as Debbie could remember. On many occasions, when Debbie's parents and grandparents went out to dinner, she and her older sister were left in the care of Silas and Nina. The girls' parents had no idea that Silas was molesting their precious children time and time again.

From the time Debbie and Beth were three and six years old, until they were ten and thirteen, Silas fondled and sexually molested the girls in the basement apartment lit only by the black-and-white television blinking in the background. While Silas ravaged Debbie's body, her sister held her face in her hands and told her stories. Together, the girls escaped to a land far away while the worse nightmare imaginable was played out before them.

Silas warned them, "If you tell anybody, I'll hurt your brother." So the girls suffered in silence.

When Debbie was ten years old, she and her sister spent the night with her maternal grandmother while her parents were away on a business trip. The elderly grandmother paused at the opened door to watch her precious granddaughters kneeling beside their bed. With arms wrapped around each other they began to say their prayers.

What began as a tranquil picture of innocence transformed into a nimbus cloud of horrible darkness. Their grandmother clutched her heart as she heard the two little girls pray.

"Dear God, thank You for Mommy and Daddy and Kevin, and Grandma and Grandpa Wilson, and Grandma James. We pray that You will protect us from Silas and keep him from hurting us and touching us in private places. We pray…"

The rest was a blur.

The sobbing grandmother rushed to the girls and held them to her breast. A few hours later, in the wee hours of the morning, their parents came back from their business trip two days early. The girls could hear their parents crying in the next room, but nothing was ever mentioned about Silas. All they knew was that the next time they went to Grandma and Grandpa Wilson's house, Silas and Nina were gone.

Years passed with little mention of the years of abuse by Silas. Like old war veterans who never mention the horrors of battle, the girls never mentioned the molestation again. However, the chronic pain of the past was an undercurrent to their total existence. Debbie felt dirty, used, and cheap. She felt like damaged goods.

Debbie accepted Jesus Christ as her Savior when she was a small child, but she had a difficult time believing He could accept her. She didn't see herself as a precious holy child of God dressed in robes of righteousness. She saw herself as a dirty orphan dressed in tattered rags. Then one day she went to a Bible study and heard for the first time about her identity as a child of God.

"I didn't feel like a holy child of God, but that's who the Bible said I was," she explained. "I read and reread that list of who I am in Christ. The more I studied about my new identity and the truth that sets us free, the more I began to accept it as true. I began to realize it was Satan who held up the picture of Silas and what he had done to me to remind me of who he wanted me to believe I was. But that was a lie. God took the truth and massaged it into my broken heart like a healing ointment. He placed a princess's crown of beauty on my head and washed away the ashes. He gave me the oil of gladness instead of mourning, and dressed me in a garment of praise instead of despair. No longer was my identity determined by what happened to me as a child. My identity is determined by what happened in me through Jesus Christ."

Debbie accepted her new identity. It was there all along, like a cloak waiting to be placed on the princess's regal shoulders. She received the robe of righteousness and now walks with the confidence of a dearly loved child of the King. To me, she looks like a queen. Debbie is one of my heroes.

What about you? Have you accepted your new identity? Are you ready to start believing the truth? God's asking, dear one, "Where are you?"

Mirror, Mirror on the Wall

Seeing Yourself
as God Sees You

Long long ago, in a land far away, there lived a lovely young princess named Snow White. Her stepmother, the queen, was cruel and jealous of Snow White's beauty. Every day the vain queen approached her magic mirror and asked, "Mirror, mirror on the wall, who's the fairest of them all?" For many years the mirror answered, "You are fairest of all, O Queen." But Snow White grew from a little girl into a lovely young maiden and, as the saying goes, the mirror does not lie.

One day the queen approached her magic mirror and asked, "Mirror, mirror on the wall, who's the fairest of them all?" Much to her regret, the queen heard the answer she knew would inevitably come.

"Fair is thy beauty, Majesty, but behold—a lovely maid I see, one who is more fair than thee. Lips red as a rose, hair black as ebony, skin white as snow…"

The queen shrieked in anger, knowing the mirror spoke of none other than Snow White, her beautiful stepdaughter. At once the queen decided to eliminate her competition. She ordered one of her huntsmen to take the beautiful princess far from the palace and kill her.

The next day the huntsman took the princess deep inside the forest, but he could not bring himself to end the life of one so lovely. So he left her in the woods, hoping the queen would think he had accomplished his mission. It wasn't long before Snow White stumbled across seven adorable dwarfs with giant hearts who loved and cared for her.

The next day the evil queen asked the mirror once again, "Mirror, mirror, on the wall, who's the fairest of them all?"

Once again, the mirror answered, "Snow White."

Realizing her competition was not dead, the queen transformed herself into a witch (which did not take much effort, I might add) and went to find the girl. When she did, she devised a foolproof plan to offer Snow White a poisoned apple that would cast her into an eternal sleep.

The dwarfs warned Snow White not to talk to strangers while they were away doing their chores in the forest. But when the witch appeared with the tempting apple, Snow White took the fruit, ate a bite, and fell into a sleep that was supposed to last forever.

As a child, I remember reading the story of Snow White and almost crying at the fate of one so lovely. As an adult, I read the story and realize it is more than a fairy tale; it is our story as well. Satan was once a lovely prince. Ezekiel describes him as once being "full of wisdom and perfect in beauty" with every precious stone as his covering. He was the anointed cherub who was on the mountain of God (Ezekiel 28:12-14). But being beautiful and wise was not enough for Satan. Pride was his downfall; he wanted to be like God. As a result, God cast Satan from heaven with one-third of all the angels (Isaiah 14:12-23; Revelation 12:4). After his downfall, he was no longer the "fairest of them all." Satan, like the cruel and wicked queen, then came after us with poisoned fruit of disobedience.

But the story of Snow White didn't end with her caught in the evil spell. One day a handsome prince came riding through the forest on his white horse. When he saw Snow White deep in sleep, he fell instantly in love with her and placed a kiss upon her lips. When he did, she sat up, blinked her eyes, and sprang to life. The prince scooped Snow White into his arms and took her off to his castle, where they lived happily ever after.

Dear sisters, a handsome prince has come into our lives as well.

His name is Jesus. Our prince has placed a kiss upon our lips, taken us in His strong arms, and lifted us out of the power of the evil curse.

We don't need a magic mirror to tell us how fair we are. The Bible is the only mirror we need. When we look into God's Word, He tells us exactly who we are, what we have, and where we are—we're spiritually beautiful in Christ. Let's take a closer look in the only mirror that matters and examine the reflection we find there.

Who I Am in Christ

I Am a Saint (Ephesians 1:1)

When speaking at women's conferences, I often ask, "If you consider yourself a sinner saved by grace, would you please raise your hand?" Hands quickly shoot up all around the room with great confidence.

"Great," I continue. "Now, if you consider yourself a saint, would you please raise your hand?" With this inquiry, very few, if any, hands go up—and sheepishly, at that. But which more accurately describes the Christian's new identity? The Bible refers to Christians as saints. Paul never once wrote "to the sinners at Philippi" or "to the sinners at Corinth." He referred to Christians as saints. He wrote: "To the church of God which is at Corinth, to those who have been sanctified in Christ Jesus, *saints by calling,* with all who are in every place call upon the name of our Lord Jesus Christ, their Lord and ours" (1 Corinthians 1:2 NASB).

"In the King James Version of the Bible, believers are called 'saints,' 'holy ones,' or 'righteous ones,' more than 240 times. In contrast, unbelievers are called 'sinners' over 330 times. Clearly, the term 'saint' is used in Scripture to refer to the believer and 'sinner' is used in reference to the unbeliever."[1]

Paul referred to himself as the "worst of sinners" (1 Timothy 1:16). But many scholars believe he was referring to his life before he met Jesus on the road to Damascus.

> Paul claims that of all sinners he was "the worst," "first" or "chief." He felt this way because he had persecuted Christ's

followers so vigorously. As far as morality was concerned, young Saul had been a strict Pharisee, living a life that was blameless before the law (Philippians 3:5-6). Yet in his case as chief sinner, Christ's "unlimited patience" had been displayed as an example to all who would believe in Jesus and thus receive eternal life. Paul's life was a powerful demonstration of what divine grace can do.[2]

That same divine grace is what allows us to be called saints.

A predominant message of the New Testament is that we are all saints by the grace of God, sanctified because we are in Christ—not because we've earned the title, but because Jesus earned it for us. We are not mere sinners who struggle to do better and be better, hanging on until Jesus returns. We have a new identity and are no longer simply a product of our past failures, hurts, and disappointments, but a result of Jesus Christ's finished work on the cross.

We are saints (by calling) who sometimes sin, but the term "sinners saved by grace" is not recorded in Scripture.[3] When you refer to yourself as a sinner, you are saying your core identity is sin. However, Scripture says, "For you have been born again, not of perishable seed, but of imperishable, through the living and enduring word of God" (1 Peter 1:23). As in the apple model, you have a new seed, a new core, a new identity, and a new confidence as a saint. A saint is not a person who is perfect, but one who is set apart.

When did you become a sinner? The first time you sinned? No, you were born a sinner. When did you become a saint? The first time you acted like a saint? No, you became a saint when you were born again (see John 3:1-21).

I Am the Salt of the Earth (Matthew 5:13)

Have you ever had potatoes without salt added? They are bland and tasteless. Likewise, a world without Christians would be very unappealing.

Salt has three primary purposes. It preserves, heals, and gives flavor. As Christians, one of our privileges is to preserve what is right and good in the world in which we live. Satan is referred to as a roaring lion. He prowls around seeking to rip Judeo-Christian values from government, public schools, the arts, the entertainment industry, and the very fabric of life. Christians, on the other hand, serve to preserve the values of our godly heritage.

Salt is also an effective healing agent. Gargling with salt water helps heal a sore throat, swimming in a salty sea helps heal a skinned knee, and fellowshipping with "salty" Christians helps heal wounded souls by introducing them to spiritual, mental, and physical wellness afforded them through a relationship with Jehovah-Rapha—the Lord Who Heals.

The most common use of salt is to add flavor, and as Christians, we add flavor to our world. A gourmet cook once told me that salt not only gives food the salty flavor, but it also brings out the natural flavor of the food to which it is added. As Christians, we should bring out the best in other people.

I Am the Light of the World (Matthew 5:14)

Jesus looked out among the multitudes and said to His disciples, "You are the light of the world." I envision a strand of Christmas lights, each adding to the collective brightness reflecting the light of Christ, winding its way around the globe. We are a part of that strand.

I worked as a dental hygienist for 18 years. Fourteen of those years I worked with my husband, Steve, and four to six other Christian women. When I think back on those days, I see our team as a chandelier of light, individual yet united to shine the light of Christ to our patients. In the reception room, scattered among *Newsweek, Southern Living,* and *Better Homes and Gardens* were *Focus on the Family, Guideposts,* and *Decision* magazines.

Steve and his assistant volleyed ideas about various aspects of the Christian faith back and forth like a tennis ball over a net while they worked on patients. Talk about a captive audience! We prayed with patients, sent them books, and listened to their family problems.

Someone once asked, "Aren't you afraid you'll offend someone and lose a patient?"

"Someone might leave," I answered. "A person can get into heaven with a cavity, but they can't get to heaven without knowing Christ."

In our own simple way, we were being light in a very dark world.

Think for a moment about what light does. It drives out darkness. Even the smallest birthday candle in a darkened coliseum will push the darkness aside. Jesus encourages Christians not to hide their light under a bushel, but to put it on a stand to be seen by all. Jesus said He was the light of the world. He has put that same light in us. It is part of our new identity.

Robert Louis Stevenson said, "When a happy man comes into a room, it is as if another candle has been lighted." How much more does a Christian who has something to be truly happy about light up a room!

I Am Chosen (Colossians 3:12)

K.C. was a beautiful blonde freshman at Georgia State University. She was excited to be at college and looked forward to having a fresh start at life. When rush week came around, she was the first to sign up. This was the week when all the girls desiring to become a member of a sorority went from Greek house to Greek house mingling and hoping to be chosen to become a "sister." After a tiring week of parties, constant smiling, and small talk, the girls waited anxiously until the Friday night party to find out who chose them. K.C. began getting dressed for the celebration when the phone rang.

"Hello," she answered cheerfully.

"Hi, K.C. This is Cassie, the rush coordinator. I'm sorry to tell you this, but looking at the list, no one chose you."

Those words "No one chose you" rang in K.C.'s ears for years.

After a conference when I was speaking about our new identity in Christ, K.C. came up and told me this story. She had never told anyone before, but now she was free from the pain of those words.

"For the first time in my life, I can let go of that pain because I realize I *was* chosen. God chose me. He chose ME. So what if those girls didn't. God chose me, and that's much more impressive than a sorority pin."

God chose you, precious sister. Like a groom who chooses, pursues, and captures the love of his life, He chose you!

I Am God's Workmanship (Ephesians 2:10)

When my son was in elementary school, he created some works of art that had a striking resemblance to that of world-renowned artist Picasso. However, Picasso's paintings are worth millions of dollars and my son's are only valuable to me. What makes a work of art valuable? Its value is based on the artist who created it. You, dear friend, are a priceless work of art created by God Himself. King David described it this way:

> For you created my inmost being, you knit me together in my mother's womb. I praise you because I am fearfully and wonderfully made; your works are wonderful, I know that full well. My frame was not hidden from you when I was made in the secret place. When I was woven together in the depths of the earth, your eyes saw my unformed body. All the days ordained for me were written in your book before one of them came to be (Psalm 139:13-16).

You are a work of art, a masterpiece, a valuable original, a one of a kind.

I Am Adopted into God's Family (Ephesians 1:5)

My friend Debbie took her 13-year-old son to the dermatologist to have a few suspicious moles checked out. The doctor asked her, "Is there anyone on your or your husband's side of the family who has had melanoma or any other types of skin cancer?"

"No, I can't think of anyone," she replied. Then he proceeded to ask a few other questions about their family history.

After the exam her son, Jason, looked up at her and said, "Mom, when the doctor asked about your family history, it doesn't matter. I'm adopted!"

"You're right, Jason," she said. "I totally forgot you were."

I love this story. Debbie went through five years of infertility treatment and two years waiting to adopt a child. Eight months after she adopted Jason, she found out she was pregnant with Jordan. Amazingly, these boys have looked like twins for most of their lives.

But the sweetest part of the story is that Debbie forgot that Jason was adopted. Ephesians 1:5 says that we have been adopted as sons through Jesus Christ. God has chosen us to be His own—we're Jesus' adopted brothers and sisters. I think that God, like Debbie, probably forgets we're adopted—He just sees us as His children.

We are saints, the salt of the earth, the light of the world, chosen by God, God's workmanship, and adopted into His family. These are just six of the many verses that describe our new identity in Christ. You are also a child of God, holy and dearly loved.

What I Have in Christ

I Have Been Blessed with Every Spiritual Blessing (Ephesians 1:3)

"I can't do it! I'm not smart enough or talented enough, and I don't have sufficient training." How God must shudder to hear His children utter those words. How many times has He heard those words come out of my mouth? The Bible says I have been blessed "with every spiritual blessing in the heavenly places" (Ephesians 1:3 NASB). With that on my resume, "I can do everything through him who gives me strength" (Philippians 4:13) should be the answer to every task God gives me to do.

I'll never forget the day I was sitting in a room full of executives from a major publishing house explaining my passion to encourage and equip women through writing, speaking, and radio. Right in the middle of presenting a book proposal, one of the directors interrupted me and asked, "Excuse me, Sharon, but what was your major in college?"

Sheepishly I answered, "I have a bachelor's degree in dental hygiene."

My mind raced back to an earlier time when a television interview showed Lysa TerKeurst and me taping our international radio program. While explaining the growth and success of the program, the commentator said, "Sharon and Lysa are not trained radio professionals." At first I thought, *He didn't have to say that.* But then I chuckled and agreed. He was right!

No, I do not have a degree in English, creative writing, radio, public speaking, or theology. But I have been blessed with every spiritual blessing in the heavenlies—and so have you.

I Have Been Given the Holy Spirit as a Down Payment (Ephesians 1:13-14)

The Peter we see in the Gospels (Matthew, Mark, Luke, and John), and the Peter we see in Acts do not seem like the same man. It is obvious that between the crucifixion of Jesus, when Peter denied Jesus three times, and Pentecost less than two months later, when he preached powerfully and led 3000 people to Christ, that Peter experienced an infusion of power and confidence. What exactly happened? He received the gift of the Holy Spirit.

Before Jesus left His disciples, He made them some powerful promises. "The Holy Spirit, whom the Father will send in my name, will teach you all things and will remind you of everything I have said to you" (John 14:26). "But you will receive power when the Holy Spirit comes on you; and you will be my witnesses in Jerusalem, and in all Judea and Samaria, and to the ends of the earth" (Acts 1:8).

Peter received that power and commenced to change the entire world. The good news is that God has given you that same power. Jesus said, "I tell you the truth, anyone who has faith in me will do what I have been doing. He will do even greater things than these, because I am going to the Father" (John 14:12).

God has given you the power of the Holy Spirit—and that's just the down payment of what is to come.

I Have a Shared Inheritance (Romans 8:17)

Imagine you have just been informed that you have inherited a multilevel mansion equipped with every conceivable treasure. You run up the curving brick sidewalk, throw open the massive oak doors, and excitedly run from room to room hardly believing the good fortune bequeathed to you! However, what you discover are not the surroundings fit for a queen that you expected, but sensible chambers, adequately furnished and sparsely decorated.

In the foyer, a beautifully carved winding staircase, adorned with plush crimson carpet, beckons you to climb to the next level. You consider the steps, look back over your shoulder, and decide, "Hey, the lower level's enough for me. Besides, I'm afraid of heights. I'll just stay down here where it's safe."

Unbeknownst to you, the upper levels house all the treasures intended to become your inheritance, and you're standing in the servants' quarters. Awaiting upstairs are a golden gilded ballroom for dances with the King, a chandeliered dining hall for banquets of every kind, four-poster beds with down-filled mattresses for peaceful rest, a safe filled with enough gold and silver to last a lifetime, and a jewel chest brimming with family heirlooms.

All that stood between you and the treasure was the staircase. What kept you on ground level? Contentment with mediocrity? Lack of knowledge? A fear of the unknown?

We all have an inheritance from our heavenly Father. We are co-heirs with Jesus Christ. But oftentimes we spend our days in the servants' quarters, never climbing the stairs to where the true riches are stored.

We can move forward with confidence, knowing that whatever He calls us to do, He will provide what we need. If He gives us the vision, He will give the provision. He doesn't necessarily call the qualified, but He always qualifies the called.

I Have Been Equipped for Every Good Work (2 Timothy 3:16-17)

Imagine with me for just a moment. Let's say you have on goggles, a wet suit, flippers, and an oxygen tank strapped to your back. Now, what are you equipped to do? I'm hoping you said scuba dive.

Now, let's say that you are all suited up to go deep sea diving and explore the wonders of the ocean, but instead you walk down the hall to the bathroom and hop into the water-filled tub. There you sit dressed in your diving gear, playing with your rubber ducky.

I hope you have a smile on your face. God has equipped us and empowered us for good works that He has prepared in advance for us to do (Ephesians 2:10). He has given us the power of the Holy Spirit, the gifts of the Holy Spirit, and the mind of Christ. Many of us need to get out of the bathtub and dive into the ocean of opportunity to explore the wonders of God's incredible world.

We are blessed with every spiritual blessing, co-heirs with Christ, given the power of the Holy Spirit as a down payment, and equipped for every good work He has called us to do.

Where I Am in Christ

I Am in Christ (Ephesians 1:4)

One of the most sought-after positions of any middle school student is to be considered part of the "in crowd." Well, I have good news for you. If you are a Christian, you are in the only "in crowd" that matters. As a child I often heard the phrase that we can have Jesus in our hearts, but I do not ever remember hearing that we can be *in Him.* Yet, for every one time the Bible says that Christ is in the believer, there are ten that say that the believer is *in Christ.* At least 40 times in the small book of Ephesians, Paul writes that we are *in Christ.* Take a look at these verses:

> Praise be to the God and Father of our Lord Jesus Christ, who has blessed us in the heavenly realms with every spiritual blessing *in Christ.* For he chose us *in him* before the creation of the world to be holy and blameless in his sight. *In love* he predestined us to be adopted as his sons *through Jesus Christ,* in accordance with his pleasure and will—to the praise of his glorious grace, which he has freely given us

in the One he loves. In him we have redemption through his blood, the forgiveness of sins, in accordance with the riches of God's grace that he lavished on us with all wisdom and understanding...*In him* we were also chosen, having been predestined according to the plan of him who works out everything in conformity with the purpose of his will, in order that we, who were the first to hope *in Christ,* might be for the praise of his glory. And you also were included *in Christ* when you heard the word of truth, the gospel of your salvation. Having believed, you were marked *in him* with a seal, the promised Holy Spirit" (Ephesians 1:3-8,11-13).

One spring our family hosted a foreign exchange student from Russia. Before he left he gave us a set of graduated wooden Russian dolls. The first one was about one inch tall and fit inside a larger one, which fit inside a larger one, which fit inside yet another larger one. What a picture of being in Christ.

Before Jesus went to the cross, He prayed for you and for me. He said, "On that day you will realize that I am in my Father, and you are in me, and I am in you" (John 14:20). Jesus in you in Jesus in God.

In *The Confident Woman,* Anabel Gillham suggests getting three envelopes of graduated sizes and a small slip of paper. On the largest of the envelopes, print GOD. On the next size down, print JESUS. On the smallest of the three, print your name. Then on the slip of paper, print JESUS. Now, put the slip of paper (Jesus) in the smallest envelope (you). Place that envelope into the next smallest envelope (Jesus). Finally, place that envelope into the largest one (God). Now you have a picture of John 14:20. Before anything can get to you, it has to go through God the Father, through Jesus the Son, and when it gets to you, it finds you filled with Jesus. "Look where you are! Secure. Safe. Sheltered. Hidden. Surrounded by love."[4]

I Am a Citizen of Heaven (Philippians 3:20)

During our foreign exchange student's stay with us, we had many challenges. His English was very limited, and we were dependent on hand signals and facial expressions to get by. On one occasion I was trying to get him to write his parents a letter. I pulled out the stationery, handed him a pen, pointed to a picture of his parents, and said, "Why don't we write your parents a letter?" He had no idea what I was talking about.

For 20 minutes I drew pictures and tried to get him to understand. Finally, with tears in his eyes, he looked up at me and said, "What do?"

I just hugged him and put the pen and paper away.

Sometimes I feel just like our little Russian guest. I don't understand the cruelty I read in the papers and hear on the news. I am confused at the angry attitudes of drivers with road rage. I don't understand how an adult could harm a child. In confusion I look to my heavenly Father and say, "What do?"

Then God reminds me that I will never feel at home here on earth because I am an alien, a foreigner. My true citizenship is in heaven, and I'm just a foreign exchange student here for a short while. I am not home yet.

Many Christians have known the saving power of Jesus Christ for 10, 20, or 30 years, but they've never understood their true identity as a child of God. As a result, they have gone through life feeling inferior, inadequate, and insecure. But when we understand our personage—who we are—that dispels feelings of inferiority. When we understand our possessions—what we have—that dispels feelings of inadequacy. When we understand our position—where we are—that dispels feelings of insecurity. We have only to look in the mirror of God's Word and discover our true identity.

A Wrong Perception of the Truth

Once there was an older woman named Mildred. Mildred had spent the entire day at a shopping mall and was leaving with her arms loaded down with packages. Upon exiting the mall, she approached the parking lot and noticed six foreign men sitting in her car. Now, I would have gone and found a security guard, but not this spunky lady. She marched right over to the car and yelled, "Get out of my car!"

The six men probably could not understand English and simply turned their heads in the opposite direction. What do you do when someone can't speak English? Well, in the South, we say it louder.

"Get out of my car this instant!" Mildred yelled.

Again, they turned their heads, ignoring her.

Mildred's husband was a retired state patrolman. He had taught her how to use a gun and insisted that she carry one at all times. She calmly put down her packages, pulled out the gun, and tapped one of the men on his shoulder through an opened window.

"I said, get out of my car!" she yelled once again.

They might not have understood English, but the gun they understood. She said she had never seen six men run so fast!

Satisfied, Mildred picked up her packages, opened the passenger side door, and placed her packages on the front seat. Then she took her key out of her pocketbook and proceeded to place it in the ignition. Suddenly, she had a sinking feeling in her stomach, as she noticed many things in the car that did not look familiar to her. She tried to insert the key in the ignition, but it would not fit. It was then she realized—this was not her car!

Mildred jumped out of the car and found hers several rows over. She never saw those six men again.

Mildred had the right key, didn't she? But the problem was, she was in the wrong car. She had a wrong perception of the truth.

Every Christian has the key to the ultimate makeover—it is having a personal and ongoing relationship with Jesus Christ. But many are trapped with a wrong perception of the truth. Many are stuck in the parking lot of life, not able to move forward. They are holding the right key but wondering why they can't get on with their journey to becoming conformed to the image of Christ. If you are feeling stagnant in your journey, perhaps you have a wrong perception of the truth.

God's Word tells us who we are, what we have, and where we are in Christ. Through Christ, you are the fairest of them all because when God looks at you, He sees His Son. And remember—the mirror (God's Word) doesn't lie.

Unshakable Confidence

Overcoming Inferiority, Insecurity, and Inadequacy

It was a crisp fall weekend in the rolling hills of Ohio. The leaves had just put on their scarlet, auburn, and burnt orange party dresses for the season, and the first frost had dusted the grassy hills like confetti for a grand celebration. Yes, change was in the air.

I was speaking to a group of women for their annual fall retreat. The committee had worked for months preparing the decorations, planning the food, and praying a covering of protection over each potential attendee. The theme for the weekend was "Unveiling the Bride of Christ," and several of the women had displayed their satin, lace, and pearl-studded wedding gowns on mannequins across the stage. A rose arbor at the entrance of the sanctuary gave the allusion that each participant was indeed a beautiful bride as she passed under the arches and down the red-carpeted aisle. A guest registry with a white-plumed pen recorded honored guests as they arrived. The Bible passage for the weekend was printed on the program.

> Whenever anyone turns to the Lord, the veil is taken away. Now the Lord is the Spirit and where the Spirit of the Lord is, there is freedom. And we, who with unveiled faces all reflect the Lord's glory, are being transformed into his likeness with ever increasing glory, which comes from the Lord, who is the Spirit (2 Corinthians 3:16-18).

Amanda was among the leadership team who was praying for the spiritual veil to be lifted from those attending the conference. Little did she know, one of the veils to be lifted would be her own.

In elementary school Amanda emerged as a leader among her peers. She was constantly surrounded by admiring classmates and praised by adoring teachers as she excelled in every subject. Even as a young child, Amanda showed great promise as a musician, learning to play various instruments with ease and fluidity.

Amanda moved into middle school with bold confidence in her abilities as a student, talents as a musician, and charisma as a leader. However, unlike in her smaller elementary school, she was not at the top of her class scholastically, nor did she shine socially. She struggled in her schoolwork and in making friends. Her grades went down, her weight went up, and her confidence plummeted.

"I don't know what happened exactly," Amanda said. "I felt as though someone had snuck in and stolen my confidence. I wasn't doing well in school, which led me to believe I had lost my ability to do so. I remember one of my teachers saying, 'Amanda, your writing is excellent. You express yourself beautifully on paper. But the minute you open your mouth, you're an accident waiting to happen.' From that time on, I never spoke up in class again. I felt stupid and ditzy, and I feared I would say something in class to confirm my teacher's estimation of me.

"My sinking self-esteem also affected one of my greatest passions—playing musical instruments. Because I made mistakes and fumbled with the notes, I decided I had no talent. After a while I put my flute in its case and stored it in the back of my closet along with many of my hopes and dreams. I had no talent, so why try? I also closed the wooden cover over my piano keys, and the melodious sounds that once filled my parents' home fell silent.

"I was the youngest of four children. During this same period of time, two brothers and one sister left home for college and careers. One brother was a medical doctor in a hospital overseas, one worked for the government in international trade, and my sister was studying concert piano and voice in a major university. Then there was me—a loser."

Amanda told me she felt like a failure at every turn, living in the shadow of her successful siblings. All she wanted to be was a wife and mother. In her parents' eyes that was not enough, and they were disappointed that she had no ambition or drive to succeed. She also felt they would be glad when she was "out of their hair."

During her junior year in high school, Amanda recalls the sting of a conversation she overheard among her parents and their friends.

"Next year you'll be empty-nesters. Can you believe it?" the friend said.

"Oh, we're kind of looking forward to it," her parents replied.

Actually, during her last two years of high school, they acted as if they already were empty nesters—leaving Amanda at home alone for long periods of time while they traveled on business trips around the world.

Dejected and alone, Amanda felt inferior to her brothers and sister, inadequate as a student and a woman, and insecure with no one who loved her just because of who she was. However, during her first year of college, she met a young man who spoke words of love and promise. When he proposed, she said yes, because she didn't know what else to do with her life. Even though her parents urged the two young people to wait and not drop out of college, Amanda grabbed at her chance for happiness and love before it had a chance to slip away.

Amanda explained, "As I walked down the aisle on my wedding day, the day that should have been the happiest day of my life, I felt like a failure and a disappointment to my family. I entered marriage as a wounded individual with self-esteem so low, there was no way I could be a helper to someone else."

It wasn't long before Amanda's husband began to make comments that she was stupid and a poor excuse for a wife. She believed him.

After their first year of marriage, Amanda heard the gospel for the first time and immediately accepted Jesus Christ as her Savior. What a balm it was to know there *was* someone who loved her just the way she was—someone who valued her as a person. However, those feelings of inferiority, insecurity, and inadequacy still ruled her life and her emotions. She had very little confidence as a wife, mother, or a child of God.

During the weekend retreat, God opened Amanda's eyes to the truth of Scripture. She saw that she was a dearly loved child of God who has been blessed with every spiritual blessing in the heavenly places. She saw for the first time that it was Satan's lies that kept her in bondage to feelings of worthlessness. It was the enemy who told her she was stupid, unlovely, unworthy, and a failure. But that was not the truth at all. It was lies, all lies.

"I learned that the Bible said I am chosen, I am holy, I am dearly loved, I have the mind of Christ, and I can do all things through Christ who gives me strength. I may not have my PhD, I may not have a college degree, but my name is written in the Lamb's book of life, and that is the only credential I need."

Also at the retreat, I encouraged the women to go back to the enemy's camp and take back what he had stolen from them. In 1 Samuel 30, we read about a time when King David's enemies attacked his camp and stole his and his men's wives and children. The men wept until they had no strength left to weep, and some threatened to stone him. King David did not accept defeat. He strengthened himself in the Lord and rallied several hundred of his fighting men to prepare for battle. David's men confidently marched into the enemy's camp and took back what they had stolen from them. Likewise, we have an enemy who has stolen from us. John 10:10 describes Satan as an enemy who comes to steal, kill, and destroy. He attempts to steal our peace, our joy, and our dreams. Like King David and his mighty men, we need to go to the enemy's camp and take back what he has stolen from us.

After the retreat, Amanda decided to go home and do just that.

The next day she opened her closet, reached back through the clutter, and pulled out her flute. With newfound confidence in Christ, she placed it to her lips, closed her eyes, and began playing as she had never played before. Heavenly music filled her home and her heart. God restored her confidence, her ability, and her talent, which the enemy's lies had stolen many years before. Amanda then uncovered the piano keys and her nimble fingers played as if she were a practiced musician. Silent notes sprang to life at her fingertips.

Amanda's transformation was phenomenal. I must tell you that she is one of the most beautiful women I have ever met. No one would have ever guessed that she felt unconfident, unattractive, unlovable, unintelligent, untalented, and unworthy. But when Amanda found out who she is in Christ, what she has in Christ, and where she is in Christ, she experienced a "confidence makeover." She truly glows with the radiance of Christ. Now when Amanda hears destructive criticism aimed at belittling her abilities or devaluing her as a person, she reminds herself, "God says that I am chosen, dearly loved, the salt of the earth, the light of the world, clothed with righteousness and equipped with the mind of Christ! And He always tells the truth."

Amanda had a confidence makeover. You can have one too!

The Barbie Syndrome

Psychologist Dr. James Dobson notes that lack of self-esteem is one of the greatest problems among women today, and it's easy to see why.[1] It's not easy being a girl. We are expected to be Martha Stewart in the kitchen, Mother Teresa in the community, Angelina Jolie in the gym, Oprah Winfrey in the boardroom, and Catherine Zeta-Jones in the bedroom—all while looking fit, fresh, and firm forever. The media spends so much time trying to define women's roles we've lost God's perspective on one of His most amazing creations— woman. In this beauty- and youth-oriented culture, she's expected to remain boundlessly beautiful, seductively slender, and agelessly active her entire life. These expectations are causing women everywhere to feel as though they don't measure up, they can't quite cut it, and they aren't the women society expects them to be. As the media attempts to push the modern woman in these directions, she has found herself feeling disheartened, dissatisfied, and discontented.

Before teaching a seminar on the unrealistic expectations placed on women today, I decided to find a visual icon to make a lasting impression on my audience, so I visited the local toy store. My desire was to buy a Barbie. I have a grown son, and I had not walked down those pink aisles in the toy store in quite some time. I was surprised to discover that you don't simply go to a toy store and buy *a* Barbie. There are hundreds of different types of Barbies. I was amazed to discover all this little lady had accomplished in the past 25 years or so since I had seen her last. I had known Barbie when she was simply a regular doll with a nice figure, some smashing party clothes, a handsome boyfriend named Ken, and an orange convertible with teal interior. But she's come a long way, baby, and here are just a few of her accomplishments. She's now a dentist, surgeon, veterinarian, cheerleader, animal rights activist, professional basketball player for the WNBA, child care worker, store clerk, Olympic gymnast, aerobics instructor, race car driver, and soldier—just to name a few. She even has her own web page. Alas, in the year 2000 we received the wonderful news that Barbie was running for political office with the debut of President Barbie. I feel like an underachiever just thinking about it.

Not only has she managed to accomplish formidable achievements, she has remained glamorous, gorgeous, and sexy at the same time. If you blew Barbie up to life size, her measurements would be 38-18-34 and she would be six feet tall. Maybe I don't travel in the right circles, but I don't know many women who fit that description. The only blemish I could find on Barbie was the "made in Japan" stamped on the bottom of one of her otherwise perfect feet. No wonder little girls grow up feeling inferior, insecure, and inadequate.

The pressure to do it all and look glamorous while doing it doesn't end in the pink aisle of the toy store. This message is also splashed on high-rise billboards, plastered on slick magazines, aired on nightly television, enlarged on the silver screen, and promoted on the elementary school playground.

When I was newly married, I went to hear a speaker talk about how to be the "total woman." She had some very interesting ideas, especially some creative uses for Saran Wrap. However, as I looked around at the women in the room, there were more who looked like the "totaled woman" than the "total woman." Someone reading this might say, "Well, those girls just need to get into church!" But the problem was, we were in church. Most of the women knew Jesus as Savior, but the peace, joy, and contentment He offers were a distant dream rather than a daily reality.

Instead of being "oaks of righteousness, a planting of the LORD" as Isaiah 61:3 describes, we looked more like Charlie Brown's Christmas tree—sparse, limp, and bent over trying to bear the weight of a single ornament. Sure, we can decorate the tree and make it beautiful on the outside, just like Sally, Linus, Snoopy, and Pigpen decorated Charlie Brown's little tree. But we know what lies underneath the glitter, tinsel, and twinkling lights.

You can't walk through the grocery store checkout line without being reminded of how insecure women feel today. Magazine racks overflow and bookstore shelves bulge with authors telling us how to boost our confidence and become more assertive, assured, and positive individuals. For example, *Self* magazine featured an article titled "Shortcuts to Confidence: Small Skills, Big Rewards."[2] Basically, the writer said in order to feel confident—fix something. That's right—fix something. She had a lazy Susan. It was broken. She got a Phillips head screwdriver. Fixed it. And she felt triumphant, competent, and empowered. I don't know about you, but it's going to take more than repairing a lazy Susan to make me feel confident.

Good Housekeeping featured an article on the "Goldie Rules: Words of Wisdom for Women on How to Be Confident, Loving, and Lovable According to Goldie Hawn."[3] *Woman's Day* included an article called "Boost Your Confidence: 15 Ways to Feel Great."[4] *YM* magazine for young teens featured an article titled "Confidence Makeovers: 15 Ways to Feel Fab About Yourself."[5]

Salon Ovations magazine included an article titled "Super Confidence and How to Get It."[6] The author encouraged readers to never use the word "fail." "Super confident people simply don't think about failure—they don't even use the word. They use the words *glitch, bungle,* or *setback* instead. Super confident people privately praise themselves for a job well done. They speak firmly and clearly and look the boss in the eye when they mention the five thousand dollar raise."[7] She then tells us to make a tape of "I am" statements and play them in the morning when you get up, in the car on the way to work, on your way home from work, and before you go to bed in the evening. The tape is to contain statements such as "I am glad to be me," "I am confident," and "I am creating the perfect relationship."[8]

These ideas are like the "cheap nails" I mentioned in chapter 1. If we choose to implement these types of ideas in order to build our self-confidence, we will probably fall apart when the strong winds of adversity blow our way. I believe the only way to have true confidence is to know that you are deeply loved, unconditionally accepted, and fully pleasing to God.

The Three-Headed Monster

I see three emotions that block women from being all God intends for them to be and from accomplishing all that God intends for them to accomplish: inferiority, insecurity, and inadequacy. I hear women make comments such as *I can't do that. I wish I were talented like Sarah. If people really knew me, they wouldn't like me. I'm not very smart. I feel like a failure. I can't do anything right. I could never stand up in front of anyone and speak. I believe the Bible works for her, but I don't believe it would work for me. I don't fit in anywhere. Nobody loves me.*

Where do these feelings come from? From the time we are born, we receive messages about ourselves. These messages are programmed into our minds just like words are programmed into a computer. We may not realize our minds are being programmed, but it happened as sure as I'm typing these words on my computer. Either we felt esteemed, encouraged, and embraced as a child or we felt unloved, discouraged, and devalued. Messages were given both intentionally and unintentionally by family, friends, teachers, and other significant people who made up our little world. They were programmed into our minds and formed a type of filter or grid system. Every thought we have, every piece of information we receive must pass through that filter before it is processed by our minds. A false filter distorts the truth.

For example, little Mari was told at an early age that she was stupid, ugly, and clumsy. Her ears looked like wings, her teeth looked like a 20-car pileup, and her legs looked like a flamingo's. In the fourth grade she got Coke-bottle glasses, and kids called her "four-eyes" on the playground when teachers weren't close enough to hear. One day in geography class, the room erupted with laughter when she incorrectly answered that Philadelphia was our nation's capital.

Seven years later, as a high school junior, Mari's head has grown to catch up with her ears, the orthodontist has done a stellar job of providing her with perfectly aligned white teeth, and blue contact lenses accentuate the aquamarine hue of her eyes. She is inducted into the National Honor Society and scores 1520 on her SAT. And yet, when Mari walks into a room full of people, she feels like that awkward fourth grader with the big ears, skinny legs, and thick glasses who was laughed at in geography class. Even though she is a beautiful, intelligent young lady, that negative self-degrading filter is still in place, and deception is the glue that holds it there. She does not see herself for who she really is.

Now let's pretend that Mari goes to a church retreat and hears the good news of Jesus Christ for the first time. Let's say she makes a profession of faith, accepts Jesus as her Savior, and begins the journey of making Him Lord of every aspect of her life. What happens to the negative filter that is cemented over her mind? Does it immediately disappear when she becomes a Christian? No, it does not. As a matter of fact, she probably doesn't even know it is there. Even though Mari is a beloved child of God, holy and dearly loved, unless she removes the negative filter by renewing her mind, she will most likely continue to feel inferior, insecure, and inadequate. Only now she may heap guilt on top of all that for not feeling more victory and peace in her new Christian faith.

When Mari became a Christian, was spiritually transformed. She just didn't know it. It reminds me of a story I heard about two boys arguing if a chicken running around the barnyard with his head cut off was dead or alive. While they were watching this strange phenomenon, an old wise farmer walked up.

"Sir," the boys asked. "Is that headless chicken running around dead or alive?"

The old farmer scratched his chin and pondered the situation. Finally he spoke, "Well, best I figure, that chicken is dead, but he just don't know it yet."

That pretty much describes many Christians. It described me for about 15 years of my life after I became a born-again Christian. My old self was dead; I just didn't know it yet. I had the Spirit of Jesus Christ living in and through me; I just didn't know it yet. I was a saint, the salt of the earth, holy and dearly loved; I just didn't know it yet.

A New Identity

Paul said, "If anyone is in Christ, he is a new creation; the old is gone, the new has come!" (2 Corinthians 5:17). At the moment of salvation, our *zoe* life is restored and our dead spirit springs to life in Christ. Now we need to change our self-perception and begin to see ourselves as God sees us—we need to renew our minds and live in the confidence of our new identity as a child of God.

Scripture says, "Forget the former things; do not dwell on the past. See, I am doing a new thing! Now it springs up; do you not perceive it? I am making a way in the desert and streams in the wasteland" (Isaiah 43:18-19). Your life before Christ may have been like a desert wasteland, but Jesus brings streams of living water to course through your weary veins.

When we become a Christian, every one of those verses describing our new identity in chapter 3 are true. So how do we start acting as though we believe the truth? How do we transform our minds and change those feelings of inferiority, insecurity, and inadequacy into feelings of confidence, competence, and completeness? How do we remove the deceptive filter and replace it with the truth?

John 8:31-32 holds the key to unlocking the prison doors that hold many captive to feelings of inferiority, insecurity, and inadequacy. "If you abide in My word, then you are truly disciples of Mine; and you shall know the truth, and the truth shall make you free" (NASB). To "abide" does not mean simply reading the Bible for information, as a textbook. There have been many Bible scholars who have read the Bible for years but who did not have a personal relationship with Jesus Christ, nor did they experience the regenerative, restorative power of the Holy Sprit. "Abide" means to continue in, to remain in, to dwell in, to stand in, to tarry on, to pursue in order to experience.[9] When we abide in God's Word, the old destructive, degrading, deceptive filter will be removed piece-by-piece, thread-by-thread, and our minds will be renewed. When we begin to see ourselves as God sees us, we will experience unshakable confidence in Christ.

As I mentioned before, many people are trying to become what they already are in Christ. While our spirits come alive and our new identity is completely in effect the moment we accept Christ, the Bible makes it clear that we get to take part in the ultimate makeover process. "Continue to work out your salvation with fear and trembling, for it is God who works in you to will and to act according to his good purpose" (Philippians 2:12-13). We can view the words "work out" as exercising our faith and what we know to be true. Paul continues with this idea, "I do not consider myself yet to have taken hold of it. But one thing I do: Forgetting what is behind and straining toward what is ahead, I press on toward the goal to win the prize for which God has called me heavenward in Christ Jesus" (Philippians 3:13-14). Notice the words "straining" and "press on." It is God who transforms us, but in His sovereignty, He invites us to participate in the process through daily decisions of obedience and faith.

Remember that article in the *Salon Ovations* magazine about making a tape of "I am" statements and playing them when you get up in the morning, on your way to work, on your way home from work, and before you go to bed at night? The "I am" statements were a bit silly, but the method has some merit. The idea is found in the Old Testament as a method for teaching children God's laws. "These commandments that I give you today are to be upon your hearts. Impress them on your children. Talk about them when you sit at home and when you walk along the road, when you lie down and when you get up. Tie them as symbols on your hands and bind them on your foreheads. Write them on the doorframes of your houses and on your gates" (Deuteronomy 6:6-9).

I suggest making a list of your new identity in Christ and reading it often. You may not want to post it on the doorframe of your house or bind it on your forehead, but your bathroom mirror, refrigerator door, and car dashboard would work just fine.

Psychologists agree that we tend to act according to how we see ourselves. If you see yourself as a failure, you will most likely go through life expecting yourself to fail. If you see yourself as a sinner, you will go through life expecting yourself to continue to sin because that's just who you are. If you see yourself as a saint, chosen by God and dearly loved, you will tend to walk in confidence. Proverbs 23:7 says, "As he thinks within himself, so he is" (NASB). "No one can consistently behave in a way that is inconsistent with how he perceives himself."[10]

One night a little boy ran up the stairs and crawled into bed. After a few minutes, his mother heard a loud thump on the floor. She ran up the stairs and burst into her son's room. Seeing him in a heap on the floor, she asked, "Son, what happened?"

"I don't know," he replied. "I guess I stayed too close to where I got in."

I fear that many have "stayed too close to where they got in." Many have walked the aisle at a church service, signed a commitment card at a revival, or accepted Christ in the quiet of their own home but then never continued to mature spiritually. They live as though they are the same insecure person they were before they were born again and received the power of the Holy Spirit.

Living Below the Bar

Paul tells us "we are God's workmanship, created in Christ Jesus to do good works, which God prepared in advance for us to do" (Ephesians 2:10). But many of us don't have the *confidence* to do what God has planned for us to do. Mephibosheth was such a man. He was the grandson of King Saul and the son of Prince Jonathan, but he lived like a pauper. When he was a boy, his nurse dropped him while fleeing from their enemies. As a result, he was crippled in both feet (2 Samuel 9).

When David took over as king of Israel, he wanted to know if there was anyone in Jonathan's household to whom he could show kindness. Jonathan had been David's best friend, and David loved Jonathan as a brother. A servant told David about the crippled Mephibosheth, and he was summoned immediately. Mephibosheth lived in a place called Lo Debar (meaning a pastureless land).

My own (very unofficial) translation of Lo Debar is "below the bar." Mephibosheth was living below the bar. He was the grandchild of a king, but he was living in a pastureless land like a pauper. When he came before King David, he said, "What is your servant, that you should notice a dead dog like me?" (verse 8).

David didn't even answer him. He simply turned to his servant and commanded that all the land that had been Saul's be given back to his grandson and that Mephibosheth should eat at the king's table every day.

Perhaps you are walking around, crippled, because of something that has happened to you as a child. Perhaps you feel like a "dead dog." And yet God is looking for ways to bless you, to restore what has been taken away, and invite you to feast at His table every day. Mephibosheth was a grandchild of King Saul and potential heir to the throne. However, he saw himself as nothing more than a "dead dog," unworthy to receive even the smallest crumb of kindness from David. David's desire was to restore to Mephibosheth all the land that would have been his inheritance and invite him to feast at his table daily. Mephibosheth didn't see himself as he really was. In reality, he was royalty.

"A dead dog?"

I think not.

The Three-Headed Monster Rears His Ugly Head

The three-headed monster of inferiority, insecurity, and inadequacy can paralyze a Christian into inactivity and leave him or her sitting on the bench during the game of life…afraid to get into the game. God's desire is to destroy the monster with the truth and render him impotent in our lives. Satan's desire is to feed him with lies and train him to control our lives. Whom are we going to believe?

Believing who we are in Christ destroys feelings of inferiority. Believing where we are in Christ destroys feelings of insecurity. Believing what we have in Christ destroys feelings of inadequacy. What a transformation when a Christian believes the truth. She experiences a confidence makeover!

I do not want you to think I am always victorious and never struggle with the three-headed monster. He still rears his ugly head every now and then. Let me give you one example.

It was my first large speaking engagement to about 450 women. My topic was "Unshakable Confidence in Christ." Two weeks before I was to speak to the group, I attended a luncheon. Two ladies whom I did not know were sitting at my table, and they were talking about a speaker they had recently heard at the church where I would be speaking in a few weeks.

"He was the most powerful speaker I have ever heard," one said.

"I cried all the way through his testimony. Just to think, he had to live with the fact that his son was an arsonist. Oh, how God has worked mightily in the family. The pastor was so moved, he asked him to speak at the Sunday night service. That is highly unusual. I don't think we will ever have a speaker that good again."

On and on they sang the praises of this mighty man of God. They used words like "dynamic," "powerful," "electric," and "eloquent." I didn't mention that I was the speaker for their next meeting. At that point, I wasn't so sure I would be.

As I listened to the ladies, my throat constricted, the tea sandwiches clung to the roof of my mouth, and my heart pounded wildly. Then Satan, the gatekeeper for the three-headed monster, let him out.

"Who do you think you are, going to speak at this event? Listen to the caliber of people they bring in. This man came from all the way across the country. You are just from across town. What could you possibly have to say to help these women? If I were you, I'd bow out now before you embarrass yourself."

You know what? Even though I knew it was the enemy whispering in my ear, I started to believe him. After all, what he was saying made a lot more sense than the "I am" statements taped on my refrigerator door.

After the luncheon I decided to go by the church to purchase a tape of the previous speaker just to see what I was going to be compared to. I walked into the church, paid my $5.00, popped the tape in the console, and braced myself for the hour of power.

Nothing happened.

I fast-forwarded the tape.

Nothing happened.

I flipped the tape over.

Nothing happened. The tape was blank.

At that moment, I did not hear the dynamic speaker on the tape. I heard God.

Sharon, you do not need to hear what My servant said to these people two weeks ago. The tape is blank because I do not want you to compare yourself to anyone else. It doesn't matter what he said. I will give you a message for these ladies. I can speak through a prophet, I can speak through a fisherman, and I can speak through a donkey.

I gave him a message, and I have given you one as well. Who are you "performing" for, My child, them or Me? Do not compare yourself to anyone. You are My child, and I am asking you to speak to an audience of One.

It was indeed an hour of power. I didn't bother getting my money back for the defective tape. It was exactly what I needed to hear.

So the next time Satan said to me, "Who do you think you are?" let me tell you what I said. "I am the light of the world. I am the salt of the earth. I am a child of God. I am the bride of Christ. I am a co-heir with Christ. I have the power of the Holy Spirit. I have been delivered from the domain of darkness and transferred to the kingdom of Christ. I am chosen of God, holy and dearly loved."

Two weeks later I spoke with confidence, and God blessed us all.

Slaying the three-headed monster of inferiority, insecurity, and inadequacy is no easy task. It all begins with understanding the truth of who you are in Christ, what you have in Christ, and where you are in Christ. Is that hard for you to believe? Well, perhaps you need a "faith lift." Keep reading.

Faith Lift

Believing and Trusting God

She was among an eager group of four-year-old children crowded around my feet as I taught their Sunday school lesson. I was the teacher and they were the students—or at least that's how it started out. My pint-sized audience listened intently as I tried to create a mental image of Jesus and His disciples trapped in a thunderstorm on the Sea of Galilee.

"The winds bleeeeeeew and rocked the little boat back and forth, back and forth. The waves were soooooo big, they splashed over the wooden sides and got the men all wet. Then water started filling up the boat—and do you know what happens when a boat gets full of water?"

"It sinks," they chimed together.

"That's right," I said with a wrinkled brow and concerned look on my face. "And that's not all. The lightning was soooooo bright, it looked like fire in the sky. And the claps of thunder were soooooo loud, they could feel them vibrate in their chests."

After painting this picture of impending doom and thinking I would have my congregation just a little worried about the fate of these men trapped in a storm, I asked the question. "Now if *you* were in a tiny boat like this, caught in a terrible storm like this, would *you* be afraid?"

Then one precious little girl, confident and unshaken by the entire scenario, shrugged her shoulders and replied, "Not if Jesus was in the boat with me."

I will never forget that answer. As her words have echoed in my mind, I've come to realize that this is the answer that calms all our worries and fears. Just as the disciples had the storm raging all around them, many times the storms of life rage around us. A friend discovers she has cancer, a husband loses his job, a child is born with birth defects. These are storms with waves of emotions so high that our lifeboat fills with tears and appears that it could sink at any moment. Waves of fear rock our boat and threaten to spill us into the depths of despair without even a life jacket to keep us afloat. Storms cause us to doubt who we are, what we have, and where we are as a child of God. Waves of emotions rock our faith.

"Tell me, would you be afraid?"

"Not if Jesus was in the boat with me."

And guess what. He is. God said, "I will never leave you nor forsake you" (Hebrews 13:5 NKJV), and Jesus said, "Surely I am with you always, to the end of the age" (Matthew 28:20). Although the pain may be great, we don't need to be afraid that the storms of life will destroy us, because Jesus is in the boat with us. His power can calm the seas and still the storms of life that threaten to pull us under.

After the children filed out and scattered to Sunday lunches throughout the city, I sat in the room to digest the words of the real teacher that day. It was childlike faith in its purest form. The little girl believed God.

The Title Deed

Hebrews 11:1 gives us a wonderful definition of faith: "Faith is being sure of what we hope for and certain of what we do not see." "It is that trust in God that enables believers to press on steadfastly whatever the future holds for them. They know they can rely on God."[1] It is the "avenue through which God invades our lives."[2]

In the Greek, the original language of the New Testament, the word "faith" is *pistis,* which means assurance, belief, believe, faith, fidelity. So when we say that we believe God, we are saying that we have faith in God.

Another Bible translation of Hebrews 11:1 notes, "Now faith is the assurance (the confirmation, the title deed) of the things [we] hope for, being the proof of things [we] do not see and the conviction of their reality [faith perceiving as real fact what is not revealed to the senses]" (AMP).

I love the idea of a "title deed." That means when Satan comes snooping around and accusing us of being anything *less than* what God has declared, we need to show him the title deed, the Word of God, to prove him a liar. We've been bought with a price and stamped with the official seal—the Holy Spirit (Ephesians 1:13).

When we built our home, we were blessed with a big backyard for a playground, a shaded flower garden, and a graceful gazebo. Our neighbor's border was about 150 feet from our back door. We didn't have a fence along the border...we didn't think we needed one.

The Smiths (not their real name) had lived in their home about 14 years before we came along. Previously, Mrs. Smith had cleared and used about a third of our lot as her own. She had planted a nice ivy bed, hung flower baskets under the trees, and even had a sitting area under a big oak tree. When we bought the property, Mrs. Smith was furious that we were encroaching on her annex. But in truth, the land was not hers. The surveyors marked out the property line before we bought the lot, and even though our back boundary ran smack down the middle of her driveway, we didn't insist that they move it.

But over the following five years, the boundary line grew a bit fuzzy for Mrs. Smith. Gradually, she began to inch her way back into our yard, acting as though it were her own. At first it was trimming the bushes along the back border, then it was pulling up and thinning the ivy some ten feet within our yard. But when we drove up and saw her on a ladder trimming the lower branches off of our trees, we knew it had to stop.

"Mrs. Smith," Steve said, "what are you doing?"

"I'm trimming the trees," she said.

"We don't want our trees trimmed," Steve said.

"Well, they need trimming." Then the dam broke loose and the deluge of hatred held back over five years burst forth.

"You didn't plant that ivy! You didn't plant those bushes! You didn't plant these trees!" she yelled. "I planted them, and I can trim them if I want to."

"No, you can't," Steve calmly replied. "This isn't your yard. You can't come over here and act like it is."

"You're just selfish," she continued to rant. "What about 'love your neighbor as yourself'?" (She did not attend church, but she knew this verse well.)

Honestly, Steve and I were exasperated after seven years of a battle that continued to escalate. Finally, we did what we should have done in the first place. We put up a fence.

See, in Mrs. Smith's mind, she would not accept the fact that the property was not hers. She had used it for so long, and she had even called a lawyer to try to claim squatter's rights like in the Old West. But the land was not hers...it never had been. She was actually breaking the law.

Why do I tell you this story? Because there is someone who would like to come into your territory and pretend that it is his. Before you knew Jesus Christ, Satan used you and pretended that you were all his. He planted thoughts in your mind, sinful acts in your will, and insecurities in your emotions. But God came along and chose you to be His prized possession...His personal property. He paid a very high price for you...His only Son. And honestly, Satan was not and is not happy about that. As a matter of fact, he is furious.

Satan knows where the boundary line around your heart lies, but just like Mrs. Smith, he will attempt to creep back into your yard. He plants a little thought here, a little temptation there, and the next thing you know, he's standing on a ladder trimming your trees! Well, maybe not your trees, but he's lopping off areas of growth in your life and whacking at anything within his reach. He might even throw out a few Bible verses taken out of context.

So what do you do when you see the enemy creeping back onto

your conquered and purchased territory? What do you do if he tries to claim squatter's rights? You show him the title deed.

"Right here, Satan," you shout. "Right here in the Word of God it says that I have been bought with a price! I am no longer your property! I am God's! You have no right messing in my yard or in my life. You get out of here this instant! See that fence? That is there to keep you out. The Bible says that my boundary lines have fallen in pleasant places (Psalm 16:6), and they don't include you in my territory. Jesus owns the title deed to my heart and you have no right messing with me! You got that? Now get out of here in Jesus' name!"

The ornery neighbor eventually moved away, and we've enjoyed a peaceful existence with our new neighbors ever since.

The Assurance of Things Not Seen

Another aspect of faith is that it connects the visible realm and the invisible realm—what we can see and what we cannot see. In 2 Kings 6:15-17, Elisha's servant woke up one morning terrified because they were surrounded by a host of enemies on horseback. Elisha asked God to reassure the servant by allowing him to see into the invisible spiritual realm.

> "Oh, my lord, what shall we do?" the servant asked. "Don't be afraid," the prophet answered. "Those who are with us are more than those who are with them." And Elisha prayed, "O LORD, open his eyes so he may see." Then the LORD opened the servant's eyes, and he looked and saw the hills full of horses and chariots of fire all around Elisha.

Elisha and his servant saw the army of God surrounding them and ready to fight on their behalf. The Lord may never give us the opportunity of having the veil that separates the visible from the invisible lifted in the physical sense, but what we cannot see with our eyes is very real. "We fix our eyes not on what is seen, but on what is unseen. For what is seen is temporary, but what is unseen is eternal" (2 Corinthians 4:18). The unseen, the spiritual, is the greater reality.

Faith is not based on ignorance, but rather on what we know about God. It means believing God, even though our eyes and emotions tell us differently.

We will never have all of our questions answered this side of heaven, but if we simply strengthen our faith by believing and acting on what little we do know, we'll be mountain-moving, giant-slaying women of beauty and strength.

Faith in Who God Is

The foundation of our faith is a clear understanding of who God is. This is not based on what He does, because we cannot understand His ways and many times falsely interpret His actions. If we base our faith purely on what we see God do with our physical eyes, our journey will be a spiritual roller coaster of ups and downs, twists and turns, highs and lows. We cannot understand the mind of God or His ways. He says, "As the heavens are higher than the earth, so are my ways higher than your ways and my thoughts than your thoughts" (Isaiah 55:9). Faith is believing that "Father knows best," no matter what.

Three young men who had faith in God based on who He was regardless of what He might do were Shadrach, Meshach, and Abednego. They were Jewish administrators who served during the time of King Nebuchadnezzar. When they refused to worship the king's idols, but chose to honor the one true God instead, the king threatened to throw them in a blazing furnace. They replied:

> O Nebuchadnezzar, we do not need to defend ourselves before you in this matter. If we are thrown into the blazing furnace, the God we serve is able to save us from it, and he will rescue us from your hand, O king. But even if he does not, we want you to know, O king, that we will not serve your gods or worship the image of gold you have set up (Daniel 3:16-18).

The young men knew God could rescue them, but if He chose not to, they understood He had a higher purpose beyond what they could see. By the way, do you want to know how the story ends? The king tied up Shadrach, Meshach, and Abednego with ropes and threw them in the furnace. Then he watched them dance around in the fire with a fourth man who looked like a "son of the gods" (verse 25). Jesus showed up. The king shut up. And the men were released without even a hint of the scent of smoke. Not only is Jesus in the boat with us, He's in the fire with us as well.

The Object of Our Faith

One day I was talking to a friend of mine on the phone. Her four-year-old daughter, Hope, who was supposed to be taking a nap, came walking in the room.

"What are you doing out of bed, young lady?" Lysa asked.

"I'm having my quiet time," she responded matter-of-factly.

Hope plopped down on the couch with her "Bible"—the Sears catalog.

Unfortunately, many view God as someone up in heaven who doles out goodies, and prayer time as an opportunity to place an order. But He is so much more.

A.W. Tozer wrote, "Nothing twists and deforms the soul more than a low or unworthy conception of God."[3] Our concept of God, our understanding of who He is and what He does, is of crucial importance. Inaccurate and unbiblical thoughts about God can block His power in our lives.

In the Old Testament, there are many names of God that describe His character: He is Elohim—the Creator; El Elyon—God Most High; El Roi—the God Who Sees; El Shaddai—the All-Sufficient One; Adonai—the Lord; Jehovah—the Self-Existent One; Jehovah-Jireh—the Lord Will Provide; Jehovah-Rapha—the Lord Who Heals. When someone in the Old Testament had an encounter with God and learned something new about His character, that person often gave God a new name. Likewise, when we encounter God in our everyday lives, we will learn new and exciting aspects of His character. However, our perception of God should never be based on our experiences alone. God has given us the Bible to reveal

His nature. Through that revelation, God releases His power in our lives—power that renews our minds and in turn affects our actions and emotions.

Of all the names of God mentioned in the Bible, the one that is the most powerful is I AM. Moses asked God, "Suppose I go to the Israelites and say to them, 'The God of your fathers has sent me to you,' and they ask me, 'What is his name?' Then what shall I tell them?"

God answered, "I AM WHO I AM. This is what you are to say to the Israelites: " 'I AM has sent me to you'" (Exodus 3:13-14). That name is so powerful that when Jesus answered the questioning Roman soldiers who were coming to arrest Him with the same answer, they fell over backward! (John 18:5-6). Whatever you need, dear friend, God is.

Oswald Chambers once said, "We act like pagans in a crisis—only one out of an entire crowd is daring enough to invest faith in the character of God."[4]

Several years ago, a friend sent me a tape of a sermon by Shadrack Meshack Lockridge. With the power of the Holy Spirit oozing out of his very pores, brother Shadrack began spontaneously proclaiming various names of God. The following is part of this power-packed sermon.[5]

> My King was born King.
> He's the King of the Jews. He's the King of Israel.
> He's the King of righteousness. He's the King of the ages.
> He's the King of heaven. He's the King of glory.
> He's the King of Kings. And He's the Lord of Lords.
>
> David said the heavens declare the glory of God,
> And the firmament showeth His handiwork.
> My King is the only One whom no means of measure can
>   define His limitless love.
> No farseeing telescope can bring into visibility the coastline
>   of His shoreless supplies.
> No barriers can hinder Him from pouring out His blessing.

He's enduringly strong. He's entirely sincere.
He's eternally steadfast. He's immortally graceful.
He's empirically powerful. He's impartially merciful.

He's God's Son.
He's the sinner's Savior.
He's the centerpiece of civilization. He's unique.
He's unparalleled. He's unprecedented.
He's supreme. He's preeminent.

He's the miracle of the age.
He's the superlative of everything good that you choose to call
    Him.
He's the only one able to supply all of our needs
    simultaneously.
He supplies strength to the weak.
He's available to the tempted and the tried.
He sympathizes and He saves. He heals the sick.
He cleanses the lepers. He forgives sinners.
He discharges debtors. He delivers the captive.
He defends the feeble. He blesses the young.
He serves the unfortunate. He regards the aged.
He rewards the diligent. He beautifies the meek.

Do you know Him?
My King is the key to knowledge.
He's the wellspring of wisdom. He's the doorway of
    deliverance.
He's the pathway of peace. He's the roadway of righteousness.
He's the highway of holiness. He's the gateway of glory.
He's the master of the mighty. He's the captain of the
    conquerors.
He's the head of the heroes. He's the leader of the legislators.
He's the overseer of the overcomers. He's the Prince of
    princes.

He's the King of kings. He's the Lord of lords.
That's my King.

His promise is sure. His light is matchless.
His goodness is limitless. His mercy is everlasting.
His love never changes. His Word is enough.
His grace is sufficient. His reign is righteous.
His yoke is easy and His burden is light.

Well, I wish I could describe Him to you.
He's indescribable. He's incomprehensible.
He's invincible. He's irresistible.
The heavens can't contain Him.
Let alone a man explain Him.
You can't outlive Him.
And you can't live without Him.

Pharisees couldn't stand Him.
But they found out they couldn't stop Him.
Pilate couldn't find any fault in Him.
The witnesses couldn't get their testimonies to agree.
Herod couldn't kill Him.
Death couldn't handle Him.
The grave couldn't hold Him.

He always has been and He always will be.
He had no predecessor and He'll have no successor.
There was nobody before Him and there'll be nobody
    after Him.
You can't impeach Him, and He's not going to resign.
That's my King.

Increasing Your Faith

I remember sitting in embryology and anatomy classes in college and being amazed at the intricacies of the human body. It still
boggles my mind to imagine that a microscopic strand of molecules

called DNA determines every part of our physical body. It is also a wonder that every muscle you and I will ever have is present when we are born. (So is every fat cell!) Every little trapezius, triceps, biceps, quadriceps, and gluteus maximus—from the top of our heads to the tip of our toes—is present and accounted for when we breathe our first breath. That means that you and Arnold Schwarzenegger came with the same basic muscular equipment, but because of exercise, his muscles grew bigger!

Just as a baby has all the muscles she will ever have at birth, as a new born-again believer you received all the faith you will ever need. We are each given a measure of faith (Romans 12:3). However, some have a larger faith (not necessarily more) because they have exercised, stretched, and strengthened what they were given. When the disciples failed to cast out a demon and asked Jesus the reason for their failure, He answered, "Because you have so little faith" (see Matthew 17:14-20). This was not the quantity of their faith but the quality—their faith needed more exercise.[6] Jesus went on to say, "I tell you the truth, if you have faith as small as a mustard seed, you can say to this mountain, 'Move from here to there' and it will move. Nothing will be impossible for you" (verse 20).

All I'm talking about in this book is having enough faith to believe God when He says, "If anyone is in Christ, he is a new creation; the old has gone, the new has come!" (2 Corinthians 5:17), and "His divine power has given us everything we need for life and godliness through our knowledge of him who called us by his own glory and goodness" (2 Peter 1:3). For some of you, it may be easier to consider moving a mountain. For some of you, the mountain you need to move is your unbelief.

Hebrews 11 is filled with men and women in the Bible who believed God, but perhaps my favorite New Testament walk down the Old Testament memory lane is in James 5:17-18: "Elijah was a man just like us. He prayed earnestly that it would not rain, and it did not rain on the land for three and a half years. Again he prayed, and the heavens gave rain, and the earth produced its crops." What's so special about that passage? To me, it's not that he prayed about the rain. It's those three little words "just like us." He was just like us! He didn't have more faith, but he had strong faith.

As we renew our minds with the Word of God and then put what we have learned into practice, our faith will grow stronger. James wrote, "Faith without works is useless" (James 2:20 NASB). In other words, if we simply say that we believe something in our minds, but do not appropriate or demonstrate it in our actions, it does not bring life to us or to those around us. As we exercise our faith, it grows stronger.

My son loves lifting weights to build up his muscles. When he does a bench press and lifts a potentially face-crushing barbell over his head (this is how I see it as a mother!), he has a spotter standing over him. The spotter's job is to catch the barbell and keep it from falling on Steven's head in case Steven should slip or pick up a weight he's not strong enough to lift. As we exercise our faith, Jesus is our spotter. If we are too weak to lift the weight of a heavy load, Jesus keeps us from being crushed. If we find ourselves too weak to lift the load, we don't give up but continue pressing on and working those faith muscles until they are stronger.

Exercise the faith you have been given. Find a promise in Scripture, confess it, believe it, and make it yours. Then pick another, then another, and then another. Soon that tiny seed of faith will take root, shoot toward the sky, sprout branches, and produce a bumper crop of fruit. God's promises are precious gifts that He extends to His children. While we accept those gifts, we must always remember that the promises themselves are not what will change our lives, but the Promise Giver who fulfills them. The psalmist reminds us that "the LORD is faithful to all his promises" (Psalm 145:13), and it is His faithfulness that brings those promises to pass.

Resting in Faith

Have you ever noticed this pattern in the Gospels—the disciples get in a bind and Jesus bails them out? It reminds me of the old 1950s program *Father Knows Best*. The kids got in trouble, the father solved the problem, and then he taught us all an important life lesson at the end. Come to think of it, "Father Knows Best" would be a fabulous subtitle for the Gospels!

In John 6:1-15, we find the disciples in a precarious situation. Their lawn party had turned into quite a bash. The guests far exceeded their expectations, the disciples hadn't planned on providing dinner, and it appeared the crowd was expecting refreshments. But the disciples didn't have the funds or the food to feed them. All they could scrounge up were five loaves of bread and two dried fish. The crowd was getting rowdy, the disciples were getting restless, and Jesus was getting ready. He took the five loaves and two fish and told the crowd to sit down—He told them to rest.

Then He lifted the food toward heaven, blessed it, and commanded the disciples to hand out the provisions to those who were seated. He didn't feed the people who were running around worrying—but the ones who were at rest. To those He gave immeasurably more than they could ask or imagine (see Ephesians 3:20), with 12 baskets of bread left over.

When we believe God, we will have rest and peace in our lives. I want you to do something for me. Right now, I want you to use your imagination. Picture yourself sitting right beside Jesus under a spreading oak tree. Perhaps His arm is around your shoulder and your head is resting on His chest. You can feel the beating of His heart against your cheek, and your head moves with the rise and fall of His breathing. With His other hand, He strokes your head and immediately knows how many hairs are on your head. His breath warms your skin as it brushes past your face. Imagine Him looking into your eyes and knowing your innermost being and meeting your gaze with a warm, affirming smile, reassuring you of His love and care.

Now tell me, as you imagine yourself in the presence of Jesus, how anxious do you feel? How rejected do you feel? How worried about tomorrow are you?

You may be thinking, "Yes, Sharon. I feel at peace in that scene. But that's not reality." Dear sister, that is the greater reality. What we see with our eyes is temporal. The spiritual realm, which we cannot see, is eternal.

Faith in the Storm

The most difficult times to continue believing the promises of God are during the storms of life when the waves of emotions are so great they threaten to tip your boat and spill you into an ocean of despair.

I have been there, my friend. And I do know it can be the most difficult time to believe the truth and the easiest time to believe the enemy's lies. Let me share one such storm in my own life.

When my husband, Steve, and I decided to have children, we conceived with no problem. Steven Hugh Jaynes Jr. was born with a shock of thick black hair and long Bambi-like eyelashes that had the nurses measuring for record-breaking length. I loved being a mother more than any role I had ever experienced. Never in my life had I ever imagined so much love could be wrapped in such a small package.

When Steven was still quite young, we decided to expand our family once again.

"Steven," we explained, "we are praying that God will give Mommy and Daddy another Jaynes baby so you can have a little brother or sister."

He thought that sounded like a good idea, so he ended our family prayer time each night with the benediction, "And God, please give Mommy and Daddy another Jaynes baby. Amen."

After six months, there was no news of another Jaynes baby. I was perplexed. Then a year passed. I was distraught. Then two years passed. I began sinking in a sea of fear and doubt. All the while, Steven prayed each night, "And God, please give Mommy and Daddy another Jaynes baby."

Steve and I began traveling down the frustrating road of doctor visits, infertility treatments, and timed intimacy (which is anything but intimate). Then I began worrying about how this "unanswered" prayer was going to affect Steven's faith in God. Obviously, it was not the Lord's desire for us to have another child at this time, and I didn't know how to tell Steven that we didn't have to pray that prayer *every* night. I kept hoping he would just forget about it. But he didn't forget about it any more than he forgot the "Amen" at the end of a prayer.

So I began to pray. *Lord, please show me how to ease out of this predicament. Show me how to tell Steven that we don't need to pray for another baby every night. I do not want this seemingly unanswered prayer to damage his faith.*

We have a miniature table and chairs in the kitchen where Steven and I ate lunch together each day. One day while sharing peanut butter and jelly sandwiches, Steven looked up, and in his sweet little voice said, "Mommy, have you ever thought that maybe God only wants you to have one child?"

Shocked, I answered, "Yes, I have thought that maybe that is the case, and if it is, I am so thankful because He has given me all I have ever hoped for in a child wrapped up in one package: YOU!"

Then he turned his little head like a robin and said, "Well, what I think we ought to do is keep praying until you're too old to have one. Then we'll know that's His answer!"

What a great idea. I had been worried about Steven's faith, but all the while, it was my own that was suffering. I was having trouble believing that God loved me when He was withholding what I wanted most…a house full of children. *How could He love me and not give me the desire of my heart?* I wondered. *Maybe He doesn't love me after all.*

A favorite song Steven used to sing when he was four years old had these words:

> My God is so big, so strong, and so mighty. There's nothing my God cannot do. The mountains are His. The valleys are His. The stars are His handiwork too. My God is so big, so strong, and so mighty. There's nothing my God cannot do.

Steven didn't know how old *too old* was, but he did know God. He knew God *could* do anything. If His answer was no, he didn't have a problem with that. I told him no many times, and he understood that no did not mean "I don't love you." "No" just meant "No, because I am your parent and I know what's best for you."

The Lord taught me a great lesson through my four-year-old son. I saw in his childlike faith an example of the attitude of trust that I should have toward my heavenly Father, who loves me and knows what's best for me.

And so the storm subsided for a while. But then a tidal wave hit a few years later.

Faith in the Tidal Waves

Sometimes when I gaze at the Jaynes family portraits of three smiling faces, I can almost see a shadow of a fourth. For there are four of us, and one day our picture will be complete.

"Steve, can you meet me for lunch? I have a little surprise I want to give to you."

I was so excited to share this unexpected news with my husband that I called him at the office and asked him to meet me at our favorite spot for lunch. After five years of struggling with infertility, we had become content with the realization that it must be the Lord's desire for our son, Steven, to be raised as an only child. It appeared that he would not have a brother or sister.

And now this surprise. At lunch Steve plucked the bow from the tiny package. Nestled among the tissue paper was a small gingham baby pillow. "Does this mean what I think it means?" he asked with tears forming in his eyes.

With a lump in my throat, all I could manage was a nod that said, "Yes, I'm pregnant."

After many years of trying to conceive, the Lord had blessed us with this unexpected pregnancy. I began planning the nursery, the doctor confirmed that the baby was growing, and we were about the happiest couple on earth. But our elation collapsed when a few months later the pregnancy ended in a miscarriage, and my heart was crushed with sadness and despair. For those of us who believe that life begins at conception, a miscarriage can be devastating because it is not simply the loss of a child who is to be; it is the loss of a child who *is*.

This was a tidal wave, and it hit me broadside. I wish I could tell you I got out my Bible and began reciting the verses about my new identity. I wish I could tell you that I said, "All things work together for good" and kept my chin up. I wish I could tell you that I went into a time of prayer, trusting that "Father knows best." I did not. I went to bed and mourned for three months. I avoided church and happy people, my prayers felt empty and rote, and I allowed the tidal wave of pain to swallow my hope. Why? I listened to the lies of Satan. "I told you so," he taunted.

That's when my "spotter" came and lifted the weight for me. While I was too weak to pray, Jesus prayed for me (Hebrews 6:19-20).

One summer night, three months after the miscarriage, as I lay on my bed, crying, praying, and crying again, I wondered, *What is my child doing in heaven? What does she look like? If only I could see a glimpse of her face or have one conversation with her.* With a miscarriage there is no funeral—there are no sympathy cards. I needed some kind of closure to this grief. Then Almighty God Himself reached down and gave me a precious gift. Just as clearly as if I were reading words on a printed page, a letter was spoken to my heart. When the words stopped coming, I jumped up and wrote each precious one on paper.

> Dear Mommy,
>
> I asked Jesus if it would be all right for me to write you a letter. He said it would be okay.
>
> First of all, I want to thank you for loving me and giving me life. I remember how happy you and Daddy were when you found out that you were going to have me. I remember how you prayed that I would come to know Christ at an early age. I remember how you prayed that I would have a mission in life to help others.
>
> Mom, I know that you and Dad were sad when God decided to take me to heaven before I was born. I saw the

tears that you cried. But, Mom, what I wanted to tell you is this: Your prayers were answered. I am healthy. I am strong. I do know Christ, and He lets me sit on His lap every day. And, Mom, I do have a mission. Every day new babies come to heaven who were never born. Many of them never knew the love of a mother or father. When they come to heaven, they always ask the same question: "Baby Jaynes, tell me, what was it like to have the love of a mother?" And I can tell them. Oh, how I can tell them.

Thank you, Mom, for loving me. I know you miss me. But one day we will be together and what a time we will have. Until then, imagine me happy and whole, playing at the feet of Jesus, and telling other babies about what it feels like to have a mommy who loves them.

See you soon,
Baby Jaynes

What a precious gift the Lord had given me. The time of mourning had passed. I still have days when I long for this child. Some days when I look at portraits of the Jaynes threesome adorning our family room walls, I still see a fourth shadow in the sunlight. But there will come a day when my little girl will not be a mere shadow. I will hold her in my arms. Until then, it gives me great comfort picturing her healthy and whole and being held lovingly in the arms of Jesus.

During those months, I had to cling to what I knew to be true, rather than how I felt. Even though I did not understand or see God's plan, I did trust his heart. This one thing we can be sure of: "All the ways of the LORD are loving and faithful," whether we understand them or not (see Psalm 25:10).

Faith. It is believing God no matter what our eyes and emotions tell us. It is not enough just to know the words in our heads; we must believe them in our hearts. Faith is trusting God in the dark. It is knowing that He is in the boat with us during the calm and during the great storms of life. He loves you, dear friend, more than you could ever know.

Who's Report Will You Believe?

Faith…it's what takes us into our personal Promised Land. In the Old Testament, God brought the Israelites out of the bondage of Egyptian slavery. Moses led the people under the blood-stained doorframes of the Passover, across the dry land of the Red Sea, and to a land flowing with milk and honey. The travelers witnessed God part the sea, rain down quail from heaven, scatter manna on the ground, and pour water from a rock. He guided them by a fire at night and a cloud by day. And yet, when it came time to march into the Promised Land, the land that was theirs for the taking, they faced a crisis of belief.

"Send some men to explore the land of Canaan, which I am giving to the Israelites," God instructed Moses. So Moses sent 12 spies to scout out the land. When they returned, 10 gave the following report:

> We went into the land which you sent us and it does flow with milk and honey! Here is its fruit. But the people who live there are powerful, and the cities are fortified and very large…We can't attack those people; they are stronger than we are…The land we explored devours those living in it. All the people we saw there are of great size…We seemed like grasshoppers in our own eyes, and we looked the same to them (Numbers 13:27-33).

But two of the spies, Caleb and Joshua, believed God:

> We should go up and take possession of the land, for we can certainly do it!…If the LORD is pleased with us, he will lead us into that land, a land flowing with milk and honey, and will give it to us. Only do not rebel against the LORD. And do not be afraid of the people of the land, because we will swallow them up. Their protection is gone, but

the LORD is with us. Do not be afraid of them (Numbers 13:30; 14:8-9).

Guess whom the people believed? They believed the "evil report"—the ten men who did not believe God rather than the two men who did. God had already given them the land; the people simply had to move forward and possess it. But instead of moving into the Promised Land, they wandered in the desert for the rest of their lives. That entire generation died in their unbelief, except for Caleb and Joshua.

But when the next generation came along, they believed God and moved into the Promised Land that their parents never saw. We can be just like that unbelieving generation—saved from slavery but wandering in the desert of unbelief. I have an acronym for fear: False Evidence Appearing Real. They saw only the giants and failed to see Almighty God.

Oswald Chambers notes,

> Human frailty is another thing that gets between God's words of assurance and our own words and thoughts. When we realize how feeble we are in facing difficulties, the difficulties become giants, we become like grasshoppers, and God seems to be non-existent. But remember God's assurance to us: "I will never…forsake you." Have we learned to sing after hearing God's keynote? Are we continually filled with enough courage to say, "The Lord is my Helper," or are we yielding to fear?[7]

So here's my question to you. Whose report are you going to believe? Are you going to believe God's Word or the enemy, who tries to stop you from entering your own promised land because of fear?

Satan says, "You can't do it." God says, "I already have."

I don't want to be like those Israelites who didn't believe God. We've seen some incredible promises in Scripture about who we are, what we have, and where we are in Christ. Are you going to move into the land flowing with milk and honey? Are you going to take those promises and make them yours? Or are you going to believe the evil report and continue wandering around in the desert—free from slavery but missing the Promised Land? Whose report are you going to believe?

Renewed Mind

Changing the
Way We Think

Several years ago my family went on an excursion out West. We flew to Nevada, rented a car, and then proceeded to log in 2500 miles in ten days. One of our stops was Jackson Hole, Wyoming—cowboy country.

On Saturday night we attended the local rodeo. There we sat, three city slickers among whoopin' hollerin' locals. It wasn't hard to tell the tourists from the townspeople. There were Reeboks among cowboy boots, scarves among bandannas, chewing gum among chewing tobacco, baseball caps among ten-gallon wide-brim hats, and fringed suede jackets among skimpy nylon windbreakers. (Who knew that temperatures on a July night would plummet to 35 degrees when the sun set behind the Tetons?)

The cowboys' skills entertained and amazed those of us who thought a Bronco was a four-wheel drive. Cowboys, young and old, rode bucking broncs, raced around barrels, and conquered angry bulls. But the most thrilling event was the lassoing contest.

The moderator announced, "And now…here's the Jackson Hole High School Lassoing champion for 1997."

My son looked at me in amazement. "They have lassoing as a school sport? They do this in PE?" We all sat on the edge of our seats as the cowboy waited, poised in his saddle, anticipating the calf's release from the chute. The corral door swung open and the calf burst from the gate. The cowboy exploded through a second door with lasso in hand, and pursued the bucking, twisting, galloping animal. He lassoed the calf's neck, threw him to the ground, quickly wrapped the rope around his legs, tied them securely in place, and immediately jumped up and raised his arms in victory. As the victor stood receiving his applause, his trained steed took three steps backward to secure the rope in place. "Yup, that little heifer ain't goin' nowhere," the horse seemed to say.

The timer continued to run for a few seconds to make sure the calf was indeed captive. Then the cowboy's time was posted on the scoreboard. Time and time again, cowhands lassoed little calves, secured their captives, and raised their hands in victory. Only a few times did a calf escape the rope and make his way out the door on the other end of the corral.

I'll admit that I was feeling a bit sorry for the little calves, even though they were released as soon as the time was logged. The first time one escaped the lasso, I applauded wildly. Angry onlookers let me know with a glare that cheering for the calf was not acceptable. As I continued to watch the contest, the Lord prodded my mind and told me to look and learn. Suddenly it hit me. This event was a perfect picture of what Paul described in 2 Corinthians 10:5 when he said, "We are destroying speculation and every lofty thing raised up against the knowledge of God, and we are taking every thought captive to the obedience of Christ" (NASB).

Those calves reminded me of wild and woolly thoughts that burst forth from the stable of my mind at times: negative, rebellious, fearful, angry, worrisome, jealous, degrading thoughts that are untamed and unruly; bucking, jumping, and running wild across pleasant plains. And my reaction should be like the cowboy's: ride up hot on the thought's heels, lasso it with the truth, tie it up secure, and throw it in the dust. My response should be just like the cowboy's trusty trained horse who, because of practice, takes three steps backward to make sure the deceptive thought "ain't goin' nowhere."

Trained because of practice. Taking every thought captive. Yes, sirree. Let's lasso those thoughts, little sister, tie 'em up, and throw 'em back in the dust where they came from in the first place. Then we can raise our arms in victory with all the applause of heaven. And believe me, the faster we do it, the better.

We need to realize there is a fierce battle going on for our minds. Let's back up to the above-mentioned verse.

> Though we live in the world, we do not wage war as the world does. The weapons we fight with are not the weapons of the world. On the contrary, they have divine power to demolish strongholds. We demolish arguments and every pretension that sets itself up against the knowledge of God, and we take captive every thought to make it obedient to Christ (2 Corinthians 10:3-5).

This battle is not fought with hand-to-hand combat, but with spirit-to-spirit warfare. Every spiritual battle is won or lost at the threshold of the mind, right as the calf comes bursting through the door. Let's look at four steps for taking every thought captive.

Realize the Enemy's True Identity

On Tuesday morning, September 11, 2001, after I got my son off to school and my husband off to work, I took a long walk through my neighborhood. The sky was crystal clear blue with a gentle breeze blowing through my hair. It was a gorgeous cool North Carolina fall day with just a hint of color on the leaves. There was nothing special on my schedule—just the ordinary. However, one hour later, because of a horrendous terrorist attack on our country in New York City and Washington, DC, by evil personified, the day turned into anything but ordinary. I watched in horror as the television played and replayed the airplanes crashing into the World Trade Center towers and the Pentagon.

Amazingly, we never saw it coming. It started out as just an ordinary day.

As I thought about that, God reminded me: *That's how the enemy always attacks. When you least expect it.*

On December 31,1999, the country and the world braced itself for the potentially disastrous effects of Y2K. Families and businesses alike prepared for months for potential disaster as the clock ticked past 11:59 PM. We held our breaths, clasped our hands, and braced ourselves. Yes, we were ready. What happened? Nothing. The new millennium came without incident. And yet, on an ordinary day, September 11, 2001, when we least expected it, an evil force attacked our country as never before in history.

Dear friends, do you see the correlation? There is an enemy who seeks to steal, kill, and destroy (John 10:10). His name is Satan. He desires to destroy us just as the hijackers dove those airplanes into the twin towers.

Satan has other names—the devil, the accuser of the brethren, a liar, and the father of lies, the deceiver. A deceiver is someone who presents a lie in such a way so that it sounds like the truth. He can make you believe something is *not* true when it *is* and make you believe something *is* true when it *isn't*. He speaks in your own voice. The thoughts feel like you, because they are the old you he has memorized so well. He's not very creative, but he is very effective, and he uses the same methods with us he's used since the beginning of time.

The first step to changing the way we think is to recognize the enemy's true identity. It's not your mother, it's not your father, it's not the person who abused you as a child. The real enemy is Satan himself, and he uses your past hurts and failures as cannon fodder. If you don't have sufficient ammo in your past, he will concoct some of his own.

Once I was sitting in a group of 12 women who were sharing some of their struggles from their childhood they were having trouble letting go of. At one point, one of the ladies who had remained quiet for most of the session began to cry.

"You all have had such hardships in your life. But my childhood was wonderful. I am a terrible person, and I don't have anyone to blame it on."

At that very moment, I realized that many Christians are fighting the wrong enemy. We are placing blame on people in our past rather than on the devil, who distorts and deceives. You can't win the war if you don't even realize who the enemy is. Do not be deceived. The real enemy is the deceiver himself.

Recognize Satan's Lies

My neighbor Michael was a stand-in for Samuel, the nine-year-old son of Benjamin Martin (Mel Gibson) in the movie *The Patriot*. For months Michael wore his long hair with extensions, slipped on Italian knickers and knee-high stockings, and acted the part of an American colonial boy. He traveled to rural South Carolina where part of the movie was filmed, and he received an education in the production of a movie for the silver screen. Michael saw how producers and makeup artists made something appear as though it were real. The movie was rated R for violent content, but his parents let nine-year-old Michael watch it upon its release. The movie was a bloody, realistic reenactment of the horrors of the Revolutionary War. However, during the guts and gore, little Michael didn't even bat an eye. Why? He knew it wasn't real.

During one scene, Mel Gibson pummeled a British soldier and landed a hatchet square in the middle of his bloody forehead. I covered my eyes. Michael watched nonplused. His comment?

"That guy walked around on the set with that hatchet in his head for three days. We even ate lunch together, and he had that hatchet with fake blood glued to his face. It isn't real."

Michael knew what was true, and it removed all fear for him. That's the power of the truth.

In 2 Corinthians 2:11 Paul says, "We are not unaware of his [Satan's] schemes." So let's take a few moments and look at his battle plan. "The one who is in you is greater than the one who is in the world" (1 John 4:4), and Paul reminds us that "in all these things we are more than conquerors through him who loved us" (Romans 8:37). But let's see how this defeated foe operates and plays with our minds so we can recognize the lies when he fires them at us.

If Satan came to you in a red suit with a pitchfork and announced himself as the devil, you wouldn't believe a word he said. But he is cunning, and he disguises himself as an angel of light (2 Corinthians

11:14). When he deceived Eve, he even quoted God—albeit twisted and distorted. He has a collection of old tapes from your past and pushes rewind and play, rewind and play. Yes, he knows just which buttons to push. He also uses "I" instead of "you." The thoughts sound something like this: "I am a failure. I am a loser. I can't do anything right. I am ugly." The thoughts sound like us, feel like us, and, before you know it, we think it is us. He did this all throughout Scripture, and he still does it today.

In 1 Chronicles 21:1, the writer notes, "Satan rose up against Israel and incited David to take a census of Israel." Of course, David thought it was his own idea, but the Bible clearly states that it was not. Nine months later, when the census was complete, David felt convicted that he had disobeyed God. God forgave David, but he still had to suffer the consequences of his actions.

Satan knows exactly which lies to whisper in your ear. He has watched you over the years and is well acquainted with your insecurities, weaknesses, and vulnerabilities. Do you tend to get discouraged? He will plant seeds of discouragement in your mind. Do you tend to feel rejection and loneliness? He will put ideas that you are rejected in your mind. But are they true? No, they are not. You can do all things through Christ who gives you strength (Philippians 4:13). You are loved and chosen by God (Colossians 3:12). That is the truth. We begin to replace the lies with the truth when we take every thought captive to the obedience of Christ.

As we have already established, Satan's desire is to steal your joy, rob you of the freedom which is yours in Christ, and deceive you into thinking you are still a slave to sin (you can't help yourself) instead of a slave of righteousness. He wants to keep you from understanding and embracing your spiritual inheritance and keep you living like a pauper instead of a child of the King. He does not want you to believe the truth of who you are, what you have, and where you are in Christ, because he knows if he can, then he can keep you from being all God wants you to be, doing all God wants you to do, and having all God wants you to have. I hope that makes you a little bit mad—it sure does me.

We saw in chapter 2 how Satan came knocking on Eve's door in Genesis 3 and sold her a bag of lies, which she bought into hook, line, and sinker. He then moved on to her children—namely Cain.

Cain was not a happy boy. He was angry that God had accepted his brother's offering and not his. God confronted Cain about his jealousy and anger. Apparently it was written all over his face! "Cain, why are you angry? Why is your face downcast? If you do what is right, will you not be accepted? But if you do not do what is right, *sin is crouching at the door; it desires to have you,* but you must master it" (Genesis 4:6-7, emphasis added).

"The Hebrew word for 'crouching' is the same as an ancient Babylonian word referring to an evil demon crouching at the door of a building to threaten the people inside. Sin may be pictured here as just such a demon, waiting to pounce on Cain—it desired to have him."[1] Unfortunately, Cain did not master it, but let the evil thought turn into action—just like his mama's did. When I think of the word "pounce," I envision a lion ready to pounce on his prey. Interestingly, Satan is referred to as just such an animal. "Your enemy the devil prowls around like a roaring lion looking for someone to devour" (1 Peter 5:8). The moment we give in to temptation, Satan immediately changes his strategy and becomes the accuser who hurls accusations at us through our thought life to bring about shame and condemnation.

The good news of this battle is that the victory is already won! It was won on the cross at Calvary. Satan is a defeated foe—we simply need to recognize his lies, reject them, and remind ourselves of the victory that is ours in Christ Jesus. This is not a battle to be feared. It is a battle to be recognized and fought with the Word of truth.

How do we begin to recognize the lies? We begin by knowing the truth—by knowing the Word of God. When bank tellers are trained to detect counterfeit money, the instructors teach them by using real money. They are taught what real money looks like—the coloring, the numbering, and the markings—in order to recognize the counterfeit. Likewise, we detect the lies of the enemy by knowing the truth of who we are, where we are, and what we have in Christ. Then if a thought comes along that doesn't match up with what the Bible says, we know it is not true. We can reject the lies and replace them with truth.

Reject the Lies

Once I had a door-to-door vacuum salesman come to my house. To my detriment, I let him in. Before I could convince him I did not need a new vacuum, he had his demonstration trash sprinkled all over my foyer floor. Almost two hours later, I finally got him to leave. My first mistake was to let him cross the threshold of my doorway and enter my house. Once he was in, it was difficult to get him out. It is the same way with our thoughts. Once we entertain a thought, once we allow the "salesman" to scatter his "trash" in our minds, it is hard to dismiss it or push it back out again. The place of easiest victory is at the threshold; don't even let it in the door. It has been said, "Every spiritual battle is won or lost at the threshold of the mind." I think victory is still possible once the thought has passed over the threshold, but we will save ourselves much heartache and pain if we begin to recognize Satan's lies and reject them from the start.

Let's go back to 2 Corinthians 10:3-5 and dig a little deeper by discovering the rich meaning of some of the key words in the original Greek language of the New Testament:

> Though we live in the world, we do not wage war as the world does. The weapons we fight with are not the weapons of the world. On the contrary, they have divine power to demolish strongholds. We demolish arguments and every pretension that sets itself up against the knowledge of God, and we take captive every thought to make it obedient to Christ.

These verses tell us that through Christ we have the power to *demolish strongholds*. What is a stronghold? The Greek word for "stronghold" is *echo,* meaning "to hold fast." A derivation of that word, *echuroma,* means "a stronghold, fortification, fortress." Bible teacher Beth Moore describes a stronghold, fortification, or fortress as "anything in our lives that we hold on to that ends up holding us."[2] They are formed when thoughts or habit patterns "echo" time and time again in our lives. They are negative thoughts that are burned into our minds through repetition (such as verbal abuse) or a one-time traumatic incident (such as a rape). These thought patterns have the potential to grab hold of a mind and rule a life. We can also view strongholds as protetive walls that are built brick-by-brick or thought-by-thought. These strongholds can potentially become prisons that keep us bound rather than fortresses that keep us safe. "No matter what the stronghold may be, they all have one thing in common: Satan is fueling the mental tank with deception to keep the stronghold running."[3]

The word "demolish" implies a kind of destruction requiring tremendous power—divine power. One reason many Christians have remained in a yoke of slavery to past sins and lies of the enemy is because they swat at strongholds as if they were mosquitoes instead of blasting them with the truth as if they were concrete fortresses formed by years of construction. We cannot destroy demonic strongholds on our own strength even on our best days, but the Holy Spirit can destroy strongholds with His power even on our worst days. The power of the Holy Spirit is the Greek word *dunamius*, which is where we get the word "dynamite." "The weapons we fight with are not the weapons of the world. On the contrary, they have divine power to demolish strongholds" (2 Corinthians 10:4).

The verse goes on to describe another area that needs to be destroyed. "We demolish arguments and every pretension that sets itself up against the knowledge of God" (verse 5). I don't know about you, but on a few occasions (okay, on more occasions than I can count) I have argued with God and against the knowledge of God. Guess what? God always wins.

The Greek word for "argument" is *logismos,* meaning "a reckoning, calculation, consideration, reflection." A calculated thought might be a conclusion that you are a failure after you have failed at something. That seems logical. It all adds up. Upon reflection, it seems highly probable. However, that's not what the truth says. It is against the knowledge of God. Regardless of your calculations, God says you are a saint who has been blessed with every spiritual blessing in the heavenly places, a child of God, and an heir with Christ. You are not a failure, and you need to replace the lie with the truth.

Replace the Lies with Truth

How did an insecure little girl like me grow up to have the confidence in Christ to stand before hundreds of women and teach or write a book? It has nothing to do with self-help techniques and everything to do with replacing the lies with truth. And I can assure you, it is not over yet. Replacing the lies with truth is a continual process in my life.

The process reminds me of when I got my first computer. I was so excited when I tore into the box, followed the directions to hook up all the wires, and then flipped the switch. But much to my dismay, that was the end of my excitement and the beginning of my exasperation. Nothing worked properly. I didn't know enough about computers to even begin to diagnose the source of the problem, so I called technical support.

"Mrs. Jaynes, it sounds like you've got cross-linked files."

"What does that mean?"

"Well, what it means is that we're going to have to delete every program in the computer and reinstall all the software again."

I was terrified, but at the same time somewhat comforted by the word "we."

For the next four hours, the technician walked me through the process of emptying the computer of all the programming and reinstalling it anew.

Before we come to Christ, we learn ways to get our basic needs of significance, safety, and belonging met on our own terms. We are programmed by the world, the flesh, and the devil to live independently of God. When we become a Christian, that software is still on our hard drive. Satan has read the files, and he tries his best to keep those corrupt files intact. It takes time to reprogram our minds with the truth of God, but He is our technician. He is very patient and will walk us through the process step-by-step to guide us into all truth (John 16:13). Our part is to press the keys, recognize corrupt programs, delete the corrupt programs, and install the incorruptible truth. We renew our minds by constantly choosing to believe the truth.

Just as Satan tries to deceive you and me, he tried to deceive God's Son with lies and cause Him to forfeit His inheritance and abandon His mission. Jesus was never programmed with lies as we were, but Satan tried to tempt Him with lies.

After Jesus had been fasting for 40 days in the desert, Satan came to Him with three temptations. Just as he tempted Eve, he tempted Jesus in the three key areas of His life: His body, soul, and spirit. How did Jesus fight the enemy? He fought Him with Scripture—He conquered him with the truth. Each time Satan put an evil thought before Him, Jesus said, "It is written…" (Matthew 4:1-11).

While Jesus' temptations are similar to ours in nature, they were specific to His particular challenges. For example, Satan would probably not tempt us to turn a stone into bread; his temptations would be customized to fit our particular struggles.

It is not a sin to be tempted. The Bible says Jesus was tempted and yet did not sin. It becomes a sin when we act on the thought, accept it as truth, linger over it, or replay it time and time again. As Martin Luther once said, "You can't keep the birds from flying over your head, but you can keep them from building a nest in your hat."

Let me give you this example. I believe Satan sends us e-mails all day long (evil-mails). When we get a seductive e-mail on the screen of our computer, is it our fault? If we get an unsolicited e-mail that reads "Click here for a hot time tonight" is that our doing? Not unless you've placed yourself on some bad e-mail lists. When does that e-mail become a sin? The moment we click on it and accept the invitation. Likewise, when the enemy tempts us to believe a lie, the temptation is not sin; it becomes sin when we accept the thought as our own and act on it. Our responsibility is to delete the lie and replace it with the truth. When it comes to defeating Satan, Dr. Neil Anderson said it well: "You don't have to outshout him or outmuscle him to be free of his influence. You just have to *out-truth* him."[4]

Below are some common lies of the enemy and the truth that demolishes them. I have listed each lie in first person, "I," because that is how the enemy puts them in our thoughts.

Satan's Lie	God's Truth
I am a loser. I can't do anything right.	"I can do everything through him who gives me strength" (Philippians 4:13).
Nobody loves me.	"For God so loved the world that he gave his one and only Son" (John 3:16).
I'm not able to do this job. I don't have the right gifts.	"Not that we are competent in ourselves to claim anything for ourselves, but our competence comes from God. He has made us competent as ministers of a new covenant" (2 Corinthians 3:5-6).
God couldn't love me.	"How great is the love the Father has lavished on us, that we should be called children of God!" (1 John 3:1).
I'm so worried about this.	"Do not be anxious about anything, but in everything, by prayer and petition, with thanksgiving, present your requests to God. And the peace of God, which transcends all understanding, will guard your hearts and minds in Christ Jesus" (Philippians 4:6-7).

I'm afraid I will fail.	"Commit to the LORD whatever you do, and your plans will succeed" (Proverbs 16:3).
I'm so ugly.	"The Spirit of the Sovereign LORD is on me, because the LORD has appointed me to…bestow on them a crown of beauty instead of ashes" (Isaiah 61:1,3).
Nobody ever prays for me.	"Jesus said, 'I pray for them'" (John 17:9).
I'm a loser and so depressed. Nothing ever goes right for me.	"Praise be to the God and Father of our Lord Jesus Christ, who has blessed us in the heavenly realms with every spiritual blessing in Christ" (Ephesians 1:3).
I can't help myself.	"Resist the devil, and he will flee from you" (James 4:7).
I'm all alone.	"God has said, 'Never will I leave you; never will I forsake you'" (Hebrews 13:5-6).
I'm afraid of what Satan will do to me.	"The evil one cannot harm him" (1 John 5:18).
I'm damaged goods.	"Do you not know that your body is the temple of the Holy Sprit who is in you, whom you have received from God? You are not your own; you were bought at a price" (1 Corinthians 6:19-20).

My financial situation is hopeless.	"My God will meet all your needs according to his glorious riches in Christ Jesus" (Philippians 4:19). "Seek first his kingdom and his righteousness, and all these things will be given to you as well" (Matthew 6:33).
I'm afraid.	"Peace I leave with you; my peace I give you. I do not give to you as the world gives. Do not let your hearts be troubled and do not be afraid" (John 14:27). "God did not give us a spirit of timidity [fear] but a spirit of power, of love and self-discipline" (2 Timothy 1:7).
I'll never get through this.	"Everyone born of God overcomes the world. This is the victory that has overcome the world, even our faith" (1 John 5:4-5).
I'm not good enough to go to heaven.	"It is by grace you have been saved, through faith—and this is not from yourselves, it is the gift of God—not by works, so that no one can boast" (Ephesians 2:8-9).
How could God love me after all I've done?	"He chose us in him before the creation of the world" (Ephesians 1:4).
I'm not any different. I'm just like I was before I became a Christian.	"If anyone is in Christ, he is a new creation; the old is gone, the new has come!" (2 Corinthians 5:17).

I feel so empty inside.	"You have been given fullness in Christ" (Colossians 2:10).
God loves me, but I don't think He likes me very much.	"You are my friends if you do what I command" (John 15:14).
I wish I were talented the way she is.	"We have different gifts, according to the grace given us" (Romans 12:6).
Everybody is against me.	"If God is for us, who can be against us?" (Romans 8:31).
I'm a mess.	"We are God's workmanship, created in Christ Jesus to do good works, which God prepared in advance for us to do" (Ephesians 2:10).
I feel so condemned.	"There is now no condemnation for those who are in Christ Jesus" (Romans 8:1).
If God loves me, how could He let this happen?	"We know that in all things God works for the good of those who love Him, who have been called according to His purpose" (Romans 8:28).
I'm not having any impact on my family or my friends or the people at work.	"You are the salt of the earth...You are the light of the world" (Matthew 5:13-14).
I'm so depressed I'm not married.	"Come, I will show you the bride, the wife of the Lamb" (Revelation 21:9).

I can't help it. This is just the way I am.	"We know that our old self was crucified with Him, so that the body of sin might be done away with, that we should no longer be slaves to sin—because anyone who has died has been freed from sin" (Romans 6:6).
No one ever chooses me.	"I chose you" (John 15:16).
What I've done is unforgivable.	"If we confess our sins, he is faithful and just and will forgive us our sins and purify us from all unrighteousness" (1 John 1:9).
I just don't have what it takes.	"In Christ all the fullness of the Deity lives in bodily form, and you have been given fullness in Christ, who is the head over every power and authority" (Colossians 2:9-10).
I feel as though my prayers are bouncing off the ceiling.	"This is the confidence we have in approaching God: that if we ask anything according to his will, he hears us. And if we know that he hears us—whatever we ask—we know that we have what we asked of him" (1 John 5:14-15).
I'm too weak to do this.	"In all these things we are more than conquerors through him who loved us" (Romans 8:37).

I can tell you that it was very easy for me to come up with the list of lies because I've thought most of them myself. In order to win the battle for our minds, we must refuse the lie and replace it with the truth. After all, which column is true? Anabel Gillham has a simple idea to ascertain a thought's origin. "Add 'in Jesus' name' to the end of the sentence. 'I cannot endure one more second… in Jesus' name. I'm such an inferior person…in Jesus' name. I can handle this myself. I don't need God's help…in Jesus' name. He doesn't love me. No one has ever loved me, and no one ever will… in Jesus' name.' The source of the thought is obvious once you ask Jesus to sanction it, isn't it?"[5]

Review

Let's take a moment and review the steps to changing the way you think.

- *Realize* the enemy's true identity.
- *Recognize* Satan's lies.
- *Reject* the lies.
- *Replace* the lies with truth.

Now let me add a few more steps.

- *Rely* on God to supply the feelings. Remember, emotions are like the tail of the dog. Once we start acting on the truth, the tail will follow, but it might take a while. If you see a snake on the floor, on a scale of one to ten, your emotions and your mind shoot up to ten. But once you realize it is a rubber snake, your mind quickly settles back down to one like a pellet in a glass of water, while your emotions slowly settle down like a pellet in a glass of thick oil. If you've believed lies for more than 30 years, don't expect your emotions to settle back down overnight.

- *Rest* in knowing that the victory is yours. Isaiah wrote about God, "You will keep in perfect peace him whose mind is steadfast, because he trusts in you" (Isaiah 26:3). If you make a mistake and believe a lie…

- *Repent,* tell God you're sorry, and…

- *Repeat* the steps. Start back at the top. God's mercies are new
  every morning (see Lamentations 3:22-23).

Paul gives us a litmus test for the thoughts. "Whatever is true, whatever is noble, whatever is right, whatever is pure, whatever is lovely, whatever is admirable—if anything is excellent or praiseworthy—think about such things" (Philippians 4:8). Other translations of the Bible say "dwell on these things" (NASB) or fix your minds on them (AMP). I don't know about you, but I get stuck many times right on the first one, "Whatever is true." I believe if we could master thinking on the truth, the others would come naturally. Paul goes on to say in verse 9, "Whatever you have learned or received or heard from me, or seen in me—put it into practice." He knew that changing the way we think comes before changing the way we "practice" or act—thinking comes before doing.

Jesus said, "I am the way and the truth and the life" (John 14:6). He *is* truth. The more we think on truth, the more our minds will be conformed to the image of Christ, and the quicker we will recognize the lies.

My, my how beautiful you are becoming. I'd say you are actually glowing with the radiance of Christ! "Wisdom brightens a [woman's] face and changes [her] hard appearance" (Ecclesiastes 8:1). Stunning! Absolutely stunning!

8

Exercise Regimen

Running with the
Goal in Mind

Just the other day I was feeling stressed out, burned out, and fed up. I wasn't myself. I was unable to get anything done, unwilling to cooperate with my family, and unnerved by life's foibles.

My friend Lysa called and said, "Sharon, I've been reading a book about how middle-aged women can feel like they are losing their mind."

"Hey, wait a minute," I said defensively.

"No, listen to this," she continued. "The author said she noticed that women in their late thirties and early forties reported major changes in their attitudes, feelings, and health. Energetic and very functional women suddenly feel hopeless and lethargic. She calls it a slump."[1]

"Lysa, I know what you are going to tell me. The author says 'exercise'!"

I was right.

I have a confession to make. Under our Ping-Pong table rests an ab rocker that hasn't rocked in about five years. In our garage a Nordic Track ski machine bound with spider webs and coated with years of dust lies dormant. I do not like to exercise, and yet everywhere I turn, doctors are saying exercise, exercise, exercise! Want to increase energy level? Exercise. Want to alleviate depression and get those endorphins moving? Exercise. Want to rid yourself of unwanted pounds? Exercise. Want to sleep better at night? Exercise.

Want to lower cholesterol? Exercise. Want to decrease hot flashes and mood swings? Exercise.

So we should not be surprised that the ultimate makeover includes—what else? Exercise. I can almost hear the moans and groans now. While I don't enjoy exercise, I've come to love the type of exercise Paul mentions in the New Testament—spiritual running.

Paul—Our Personal Trainer

I can't quite envision the apostle Paul at a spa or a salon, but he literally wrote the book on how to experience the ultimate makeover. To Paul, running was an important facet in being conformed to the image of Christ, and he gave us some specific instructions on how to run well. He said, "Brethren, I do not regard myself as having laid hold of it yet; [I am not spiritually perfect. The makeover is not complete.] but one thing I do: forgetting what lies behind and reaching forward to what lies ahead, I press on toward the goal for the prize of the upward call of God in Christ Jesus" (Philippians 3:13-14 NASB).

When Steven was in middle school and high school, he ran cross-country in the fall and track in the spring. Fans cheered on the sidelines as runners sprinted toward the finish line. When running that final stretch, the trained runners knew to never look back but keep their eyes on the goal set before them. I frequently heard coaches yelling, "Don't look back! Don't look back!" They knew the runners who looked back lost valuable time.

In Hebrews 12:1 Paul tells us that we have a great cloud of witnesses surrounding us, cheering for us to run with endurance. I suspect if the heavenly veil that separates the seen from the unseen were lifted, we would hear Moses, Elijah, and the angels cheering for us as we run the great race of life: "Don't look back! Don't look back!"

In our society people waste valuable precious years looking back, trying to figure out why they are the way they are and why they do the things they do. However, Paul exhorts us to forget what lies behind. In the Old Testament, men and women of the faith did look back, but they did so to praise God for His faithfulness, never to place blame. A psalmist said, "I shall remember the deeds of the LORD; surely I will remember Your wonders of old. I will meditate on all Your work and muse on Your deeds" (Psalm 77:11 NASB). Moses reminded the Israelites, "Remember how the LORD your God led you all the way in the desert these forty years, to humble you and to test you in order to know what was in your heart, whether or not you would keep His commands" (Deuteronomy 8:2). Again he wrote, "Remember that you were slaves in Egypt and the LORD your God redeemed you" (Deuteronomy 15:15).

As a speaker, I give my testimony often. However, I am not looking back to place blame on anyone. I am telling about my past in order to bring glory to God by showing the incredible saving grace of Jesus Christ in my life and the lives of my family members.

Unfortunately, looking back trips up many spiritual runners. They stumble in the dirt because they aren't looking forward. They grovel in the dust and lose precious years because they are spending too much time looking at where they've been instead of where they are going. If I were sitting there with you, I'd cheer, "Get up! Don't look back! Keep running toward the goal! Look where you're going, not where you've been."

Paul exhorts us to leave the past behind and concentrate on moving forward toward the goal. When he says, "forgetting what lies behind," he describes it as involving the continual forgetting and the relentless centering of his energies and interests on the course ahead. "Forgetting" did not mean obliterating the memory of his past, but a conscious refusal to let it absorb his attention and impede his progress.[2]

What exactly did Paul have to forget? He had to forget the good, the bad, and the ugly.

Forget the Good

When I worked as a dental hygienist in my husband's office, my name tag did not have my last name engraved on it. It simply said "Sharon, RDH." The other staff members used to tease me about it. But the reason I omitted my last name was to prevent patients from treating me differently than the other staff just because I was the doctor's wife. Many times proud, highly educated, or wealthy men and women snubbed me as though I was just the hired help (which is exactly what I was). It always tickled me when one of them saw us together at a social function and said, embarrassed, "Oh, I didn't know you were Dr. Jaynes' wife."

The point is, it should not have mattered. I am a child of God, and the rest, as my country grandmother used to say, "doesn't amount to a hill of beans."

Paul was a man with quite an impressive resume. He was "circumcised on the eighth day, of the nation of Israel, of the tribe of Benjamin, a Hebrew of Hebrews; as to the Law, a Pharisee; as to zeal, a persecutor of the church; as to the righteousness which is in the Law, found blameless" (Philippians 3:5-6 NASB). In other words, Paul was a somebody. He was born into an elite family, studied at the Harvard of Jerusalem, and never broke a single rule. He was in the Jewish *Who's Who*—a real man's man.

And yet he decided all his past credentials were rubbish in comparison to his present treasures in Christ. He said,

> Whatever was to my profit I now consider loss for the sake of Christ. What is more, I consider everything a loss compared to the surpassing greatness of knowing Christ Jesus my Lord, for whose sake I have lost all things. I consider them *rubbish,* that I may gain Christ and be found in him, not having a righteousness of my own that comes from the law, but that which is through faith in Christ—the righteousness that comes from God and is by faith" (Philippians 3:7-9).

I love how the Amplified expands on verse 8:

> Yes, furthermore, I count everything as loss compared to the possession of the priceless privilege (the overwhelming preciousness, the surpassing worth, and supreme advantage) of knowing Christ Jesus my Lord and of progressively

becoming more deeply and intimately acquainted with Him [of perceiving and recognizing and understanding Him more fully and clearly]. For His sake I have lost everything and consider it all to be mere rubbish (refuse, dregs), in order that I may win (gain) Christ [the Anointed One].

God is calling us to forget our past achievements, quit wearing that spiritual letter sweater around the house, and keep moving toward the goal of becoming conformed to the image of Christ. William Barclay said, "Forget what you have done, and remember what you have to do." The ground is level at the foot of the cross.

Forget the Bad

First, we forget the worldly credentials and stellar achievements. Second, we forget the bad that has been done to us—the cruelties, the injustices, the hurtful words, the betrayal, the slander, the abandonment, the physical or mental abuse, the rejection. We cannot change the past, but from this point on, we can ask God to help us change what we do with it.

Remember, forgetting does not mean obliterating something from our memory. That is physically impossible unless we have a disease such as amnesia or Alzheimer's. Leaving the past behind involves forgiving those who have hurt you. To forgive and forget means to no longer use the offense against the offender. It has nothing to do with whether or not the offender deserves forgiveness. Most do not. I do not deserve God's forgiveness, and yet He has forgiven me. Forgiving and forgetting is taking someone off of your hook, placing him or her on God's hook, and putting the past behind you. It is a gift you give yourself.

The Greek word for "forgive" is *aphiemi,* and it means "to let go from one's power, possession, to let go free, let escape."[3] "In essence, the intent of biblical forgiveness is to cut someone loose. The word picture drawn by the Greek term unforgiveness is one in which the unforgiven is roped to the back of the unforgiving. How ironic. Unforgiveness is the means by which we securely bind ourselves to that which we hate most. Therefore, the Greek meaning of forgiveness might best be demonstrated as the practice of cutting loose the person roped to your back."[4]

In his book *What's So Amazing About Grace,* Philip Yancey said, "If we do not transcend nature, we remain bound to the people we cannot forgive, led in their vise grip. This principle applies even when one part is wholly innocent and the other wholly to blame, for the innocent part will bear the wound until he or she can find a way to release it—and forgiveness is the only way."[5]

What or who did Paul have to forgive? Let's take a look. He recounted the cruelties in 2 Corinthians 11:23-27:

> I have worked much harder, been in prison more frequently, been flogged more severely, and been exposed to death again and again. Five times I received from the Jews the forty lashes, minus one. Three times I was beaten with rods, once I was stoned, three times I was shipwrecked, I spent a night and a day in the open sea, I have been constantly on the move. I have been in danger from rivers, in danger from bandits, in danger from my own countrymen, in danger from Gentiles; in danger in the city, in danger in the country, in danger at sea, and in danger from false brothers. I have labored and toiled and have often gone without sleep; I have known hunger and thirst and have often gone without food; I have been cold and naked.

As I read those verses, I always wonder when and where these things happened to Paul. But he made little mention of the hardships and ill-treatment. Unfortunately, if I had suffered such treatment, I'd probably bring it up often and have a chapter dedicated to each one! But Paul chose not to record them or recount them. He put them behind him and moved on.

Paul had a choice. In the face of ill-treatment, injury, and injustice, he could have chosen to become bitter and unforgiving toward those who had treated him unfairly. But instead he chose to forgive those who had hurt him and run the race unencumbered. I believe one of the reasons for Paul's success in ministry was because of his willingness to forgive those who had hurt him.

Have you ever noticed that some of the most beautiful women with the most peaceful countenances are those who have had the most tragic lives? Corrie ten Boom was such a woman. She spent years in a German concentration camp where she was daily humiliated, degraded, and abused by Nazi guards. After she was freed, she traveled around the world telling about God's grace and forgiveness through Jesus Christ. One Sunday morning, after speaking in Munich about how God throws our sins into the deepest of seas, she noticed a heavyset, balding man in a gray overcoat approaching the podium.

And as she saw the man, she pictured the uniform he used to wear—at Ravensbruck. In a rush she remembered the skull and crossbones of his visor, the pathetic piles of dresses and shoes in the middle of a large cold room, and the shame of having to walk naked in front of this man. He had been one of the cruelest guards at the prison where her sister Betsie died. She stood face-to-face with one of her captors and her blood seemed to freeze.

The man stopped in front of her and held out his hand. "A fine message, Fräulein!" he began. "How good it is to know that, as you say, all our sins are at the bottom of the sea!" She hesitated and fumbled in her purse to avoid taking his hand.

He told her he had been a guard at Ravensbruck but had since become a Christian. He knew God had forgiven him, but he wanted Corrie's forgiveness as well.

> And I stood there—I, whose sins had again and again to be forgiven—and could not forgive. Betsie had died in that place—could he erase her slow terrible death simply for the asking?
>
> It could not have been many seconds that he stood there—hand held out—but to me it seemed hours as I wrestled with the most difficult thing I had ever had to do, for I had

to do it—I knew that. The message that God forgives has a prior condition: that we forgive those who have injured us. "If you do not forgive men their trespasses," Jesus says, "neither will your Father in heaven forgive your trespasses."

I knew it not only as a commandment of God but as a daily experience...And still I stood there with the coldness clutching my heart. But forgiveness is not an emotion—I knew that too. Forgiveness is an act of the will, and the will can function regardless of the temperature of the heart. "Jesus, help me!" I prayed silently. "I can lift my hand. I can do that much. You supply the feeling."

And so woodenly, mechanically, I thrust my hand into the one stretched out to me. And as I did, an incredible thing took place. The current started in my shoulder, raced down my arm, sprang into our joined hands. And then this healing warmth seemed to flood my whole being, bringing tears to my eyes.

"I forgive you, brother!" I cried. "With all my heart."[6]

I think Corrie ten Boom never looked more beautiful than at that very moment.

Forget the Ugly

In order to run well, we forget the good and we forget the bad. But perhaps the most difficult of all is to forget the ugly—that which has been done *through* us—the mistakes and sins we have committed.

Paul was a man who had some ugly to forget. Before his name was changed from Saul to Paul, he was known as a zealous persecutor of the Christian church. "Saul began to destroy the church. Going from house to house, he dragged off men and women and put them in prison" (Acts 8:3). He was in charge of watching the coats while an angry mob stoned Stephen, the first Christian martyr. On the very day Saul encountered Jesus on the road to Damascus, he was traveling to the high priest to ask him for letters to the synagogues so that if he found any there who belonged to Christ, he might take them as prisoners to Jerusalem. You can imagine his surprise when the very One he was persecuting opened the sky, poured forth a blinding light, and spoke his name (Acts 9:1-3).

After Saul's life-altering encounter with Jesus, his name was changed to Paul. However, that was not the only change in this man—he became a new creation.

Later he wrote, "If anyone is in Christ, he is a new creation, the old has gone, the new has come!" (2 Corinthians 5:17). To quote from the Amplified version again, "Therefore, if any person is [ingrafted] in Christ (the Messiah) he is a new creation (a new creature altogether); the old [previous moral and spiritual condition] has passed away. Behold, the fresh and new has come!" Paul knew more than anyone the joy of new beginnings. He rejoiced that he was not the same man that he had been before he met Jesus. He had a spiritual transformation and he no longer lived, but Christ lived in him (Galatians 2:20).

Have you done some ugly things in your life you are having trouble forgetting? Did you know that God chooses not to remember what those things are? In the Bible, God tells us that He "forgets" our sins and remembers them no more. But how does an omnipotent, all-knowing God *forget?*

There are many events in the Bible that begin with the words "God remembered": "God remembered Noah" (Genesis 8:1); "He [God] remembered Abraham" (Genesis 19:29); "God remembered Rachel" (Genesis 30:22); "God heard their groaning and he remembered his covenant with Abraham, with Isaac and with Jacob" (Exodus 2:24). In each incident, God remembering meant that He was about to do something—God was about to act. Therefore, if God *remembering* means He is about to act, then God *forgetting* means that He is *not* going to act. "I will forgive their wickedness and will remember their sins no more" (Jeremiah 31:34). He forgets our sins—He is *not* going to act upon them.

Corrie ten Boom once said, "God casts our sins into the deepest ocean, gone forever. And even though I cannot find a Scripture for it, I believe God then places a sign out there that says, 'NO FISHING ALLOWED.'"[7]

David wrote that God disposed of our sins as far as the east is from the west (Psalm 103:12), and yet we hop in those mental submarines and search for them on the ocean floor. I come in contact daily with women who cannot seem to forgive themselves for their past failures. Bonita, who had three abortions more than 20 years ago, said, "I know God forgave me, but I can't forgive myself." Joan, who had an affair five years ago said, "I know God forgave me. I know about grace, but I don't deserve forgiveness. I can't let it go."

I am convinced that two of Satan's greatest tools in his arsenal of weapons that hinder Christians from moving forward in their spiritual growth and maturity are shame and condemnation. In the book of Revelation, he is called the "accuser of our brethren" and accuse he does. But the truth that will set you free says that Jesus took the punishment for our sins and God has declared us not guilty. When Jesus said, "It is finished" on the cross of Calvary, the words meant, "paid in full." Our debt was nailed to the cross.

One reason we have difficulty forgetting past sins is because Satan is there to remind us of them on a daily basis. Bible teacher Beth Moore said, "He broke the chains of all kinds of bondage when He gave His life for us on the cross; however, many of us still carry them in our hands or have them dangling from our necks out of pure habit, lack of awareness, or lack of biblical knowledge."[8] We need to throw off those chains once and for all.

It is very unusual to find a woman's name in the long lists of genealogies in the Bible. However, in Jesus' lineage recorded in Matthew 1, the writer lists five, four of whom had questionable pasts. Now, if I were going to list a few of the women in Jesus' family tree, perhaps I'd list Mrs. Noah, Mrs. Moses, or Mrs. Abraham. But God had another idea. He chose Tamar, who had an incestuous relationship with her father-in-law; Rahab, who was a prostitute by trade; Bathsheba, who had an adulterous affair with King David that resulted in murder; and Ruth, who was a foreigner from a cursed country. Why would God choose four such women? I believe it was to show that there is no sin so low, no place so far, that the grace of God cannot redeem and save. In each of these women's lives, God chose them, forgave them, and used their lives to glorify Him. Likewise, dear sister, there is nothing in your life that God cannot forgive, redeem, and use for His glory.

Psalm 139 assures us that God knew every day of our lives before there was yet one of them. He knew every sin we would commit and every poor choice we would make. Amazingly, He chose us anyway.

We all make mistakes, but I hope to have the attitude of Thomas Edison after a fire that destroyed his laboratory and his life's work. "Just think," he said, "all our mistakes have been burned up and we have a chance to start all over again."

God's mercy and compassion are new every morning (Lamentations 3:22-23). God forgets the ugly we've done. We need to forget too.

Running with the Goal in Mind

In the movie *Forrest Gump,* Forrest could not do many things well, but he could run. After a series of devastating circumstances, Forrest decided to start running—nowhere in particular—just run.

"One day I decided to go for a little run," he said. "I ran to the end of the road and when I got there I thought maybe I'd just run to the end of town, and when I got there, I thought maybe I'd just run to the end of the county. Since I ran this far, I thought I'd run clear across the state of Alabama. No particular reason, I just kept on going. I ran clear to the ocean. When I got there, I figured, since I'd gone this far, I might as well turn around and keep on going. When I got to another ocean, I figured, since I'd gone this far, I might as well keep right on going. When I got tired, I slept. When I got hungry, I ate."

After a while, others joined Forrest in his "pursuit." A news reporter dashed up to him, stuck a microphone in his face, and asked, "Why are you running? For world peace? For the environment? Homeless? Women's rights? Animals? Why are you doing this?"

"I don't know," Forrest replied. "I just feel like running."

Forrest had no goal. He had no direction. He had no purpose.

And yet others began to follow and run alongside him. Then suddenly, after more than three years of running, he stopped. "I'm pretty tired. I think I'll go home now." Those running with him turned to each other and questioned, "What are we supposed to do now?"

How like the race many are running today. They run, but do not know to what end. They strive, but do not know why. Then one day, they get tired and stop. May it never be so for the Christian. We know the goal and we press on toward the prize—the ultimate makeover—conformity to the image of Christ.

Let's go back to our personal trainer's instruction: "Brethren, I do not regard myself as having laid hold of it yet; but one thing I do: forgetting what lies behind and reaching forward to what lies ahead, *I press on toward the goal* for the *prize* of the upward call of God in Christ Jesus" (Philippians 3:13-14 NASB). Paul is reminding us to press on toward the goal—no matter what.

In another passage he challenges us,

> Do you not know that in a race all the runners run, but only one gets the prize? Run in such a way as to get the prize. Everyone who competes in the games goes into strict training. They do it to get a crown that will not last; but we do it to get a crown that will last forever. Therefore I do not run like a man running aimlessly; I do not fight like a man beating the air. No, I beat my body and make it my slave so that after I have preached to others, I myself will not be disqualified for the prize (1 Corinthians 9:24-27).

Christopher Columbus was a man who understood the power of perseverance. On his journey to cross the Atlantic, he sailed day after day without seeing land. His crew threatened mutiny and begged him to turn back on many occasions. But Columbus pressed on, and each day he wrote two words in his ship's log, "Sailed on." There may be days when all you can write in your journal are those same two words, "Sailed on." There may be days when you feel like giving up because the monotonous repetition of everyday life threatens to lull you into complacency or the storms of life threaten to sink your ship. But be encouraged, my friend. God is at the helm. Press on.

An amazing example of pressing on toward the goal was seen in a marathon Olympic race. The crowd waited for the last of the runners to emerge. Hours behind the runner in front of him, the last marathoner finally entered the Olympic stadium. By that time, the drama of the day's events was almost over and most of the spectators had gone home. This athlete's story, however, was still being played out.

Limping into the arena, the Tanzanian runner grimaced with every step, his knee bleeding and bandaged from an earlier fall. His ragged appearance immediately caught the attention of the remaining crowd, who cheered him on to the finish line.

Why did he stay in the race? What made him endure his injuries to the end? When asked these questions later, he replied, "My country did not send me 7000 miles away to start the race. They sent me 7000 miles to finish it."[9]

Dear friend, God did not choose you to merely start the race. He chose you to finish it, and finish it well. You may have skinned knees and bruised elbows from multiple falls, but just the same, there will be a cloud of witnesses cheering for you when you cross the finish line and receive your crown of glory.

What is the ultimate exercise program for the ultimate makeover? Forgetting what lies behind, reaching forward to what lies ahead, and pressing on toward the goal for the prize of the upward call of God in Christ Jesus! As Charlton Heston's director assured him during the taping of the chariot races in the movie *Ben Hur,* "You just stay in the race and I'll make sure you win." You stay in the race and God will make sure you win. See you at the finish line!

Weight Loss Program
Leaving the
Past Behind

I have no doubt that I left many of you in the dust as we ran down the trail of leaving the past behind. It sounds like a lovely idea, but how do we even begin to give those burdens to the Lord that we've had strapped to our backs for so many years? Dear sisters, I know this isn't easy. It hasn't been easy for me. But you must believe me when I say that God's love and your inner beauty will never shine through if the past is a dark cloud blocking the rays. Because I do understand the difficulty of leaving the past behind, we are going to spend a bit more time examining the process. Before we can run, we need to take some baby steps and learn how to walk.

Let's go back to the track for a moment. Imagine 20 young men lined up for a footrace. They approach the starting mark and get in position. The official calls, "On your mark," and the boys place their right foot on the white painted line. Then he calls, "get set," and the boys reach down and strap 30-pound packs to their backs. Some even help each other secure them in place. Finally, the official fires the starting gun and yells "go!" and the runners struggle to make it down the lanes, weighted down with their heavy burdens.

As foolish as this may seem, that is how I see many run the great race of life. We get up in the morning, wash our faces, and then strap on heavy burdens before we meet the day. However, Jesus refers to believers as sheep, and sheep are not pack animals. They were never meant to carry burdens, much less run with them.

In contrast to the above scenario, when I watched my son's cross-country team prepare for a race, they stripped off long warm-up pants, slid jerseys over their heads, and put featherweight shoes on their feet. Because the running uniforms are so skimpy, the boys were too embarrassed to be seen in them until just minutes before the whistle was blown. But their desire to win overcame their modesty, and they understood one of Paul's greatest lessons for running well—run unencumbered. If we're not running well, perhaps we need to shed the extra weight we've been carrying around.

Paul coaches us, "Let us throw off everything that hinders and the sin that so easily entangles, and let us run with perseverance the race marked out for us" (Hebrews 12:1). Another translation puts it this way, "Let us strip off and throw aside every encumbrance (unnecessary weight) and that sin which so readily (deftly and cleverly) clings to and entangles us, and let us run with patient endurance and steady and active persistence the appointed course of the race that is set before us" (AMP).

David said, "Cast your burden upon the LORD and He will sustain you" (Psalm 55:22 NASB). Cast doesn't mean to quietly sneak up and gently lay the burden down. It means to get rid of it—to throw forcefully.

The most common burden I see among God's people today is their painful past. So let's see how to strip off the past, throw it aside, and leave it behind.

Find the Hidden Treasure

Several years ago I chaperoned a group of fourth graders on a field trip to Reed Gold Mine. The tour guide took us through dark musty tunnels, explaining how one hundred years ago the miners had searched for veins of gold imbedded in the rocks and hidden beneath the sodden walls. Many tirelessly panned for gold in the chilled mountain stream in hopes of finding a few valuable nuggets. After the tour we each grabbed a sieve and tried our luck at panning for gold.

First we lowered our pans into the mud of the streambed and

filled our sieves. Then we shook the pan back and forth, allowing the crystal clear water to flow over its contents. The silt and dirt filtered through the screen and fell back into the stream as hopeful children (and a few adults) searched for gold. Unfortunately, none of us struck it rich that day, but I did walk away with a valuable lesson.

The first step to putting the past behind is to find the hidden treasure in each murky situation. Just like panning for gold, we need to sift through the mud and silt of our pasts, allow God's cleansing Word to wash over the memories, and discover the gold hidden beneath the surface.

One of the most valuable treasures forged from difficult life circumstances is the gift of being able to use your experience to help others. Paul said God "comforts us in all our troubles so that we can comfort those in any trouble with the comfort we ourselves have received from God" (2 Corinthians 1:4). In other words, God does not comfort us merely to make us comfortable. He comforts us to make us comfort-able, able to comfort others.

Our past trials and victories give us the supernatural ability to empathize with someone going through a similar struggle. No one can help a woman suffering from the guilt of a past abortion like the woman who has received healing and forgiveness from that same past mistake. No one can apply the salve of understanding to wounds left by an abusive husband or boyfriend like a woman who bears the same residual scars. No one can wipe the tears of a mother watching a wayward teenager make poor choices like the mother who has welcomed a prodigal home. No one can minister to a woman who feels like damaged goods because of childhood sexual abuse like the abused woman who now sees herself as a holy and pure child of the King.

I see victory over hardships as a priceless treasure God has entrusted to us that we can invest into the lives of others. In the parable of the talents, a landowner went away on a trip. Before he left, he gave three of his servants talents (or pieces of money). The servant to whom he gave five talents invested them and gave the owner ten talents upon his return. The one to whom he gave two talents invested them and gave the owner four talents upon his return. But the servant to whom he gave one talent buried his talent in the sand out of fear. The master was very unhappy and took the lone talent away and gave it to the servant who had invested wisely (Matthew 25:14-28).

Victory over hardship is a treasure—a talent. Job said, "When he has tested me, I will come forth as gold" (Job 23:10). God is delighted when we invest that "gold" in the lives of others, but He is disappointed when we hide it because of fear. Satan, on the other hand, rejoices when we hide our struggles. He cowers in defeat when we take what he meant for evil and use it for good.

A Brother's Gold

In the book of Genesis, Joseph always seemed to find the hidden treasure in difficult circumstances. Joseph was the favorite son of Jacob. His jealous brothers could never say a kind word to him and mocked his prophetic dreams. When he was 17, they threw him into a pit, sold him into slavery, and told their father a ferocious animal had killed him. Joseph was bought by Potiphar, a high official of Pharaoh, to work at his home. While there, he was falsely accused of sexually assaulting Potiphar's wife and was thrown into prison. During his prison stay, he interpreted dreams and ministered to the prisoners.

Word of Joseph's gift of interpreting dreams was passed along to Pharaoh, and Joseph was called out of prison to interpret one of Pharaoh's dreams predicting a famine. Pharaoh was so enamored with Joseph's wisdom that he appointed him governor, second only to Pharaoh himself. Joseph was used to save the entire Egyptian nation as well as those in surrounding countries.

During the famine, Joseph's brothers came to Egypt in search of food. They were terrified when the governor revealed that he was their long-lost brother. But instead of ordering their execution, Joseph forgave them and found the treasure in the situation. When he revealed his true identity to his brothers, he said, "I am your brother Joseph, whom you sold into Egypt. Now do not be grieved or angry with yourselves, because you sold me here, for God sent me before you to preserve life…You meant evil against me, but God meant it for good in order to bring about this present result, to preserve many people alive" (Genesis 45:4-5; 50:20 NASB). When Joseph's first son was born, he named him Manasseh, which means "one who causes to forget." But when his second son was born, he named him Ephraim, "God has made me *fruitful* in the land of my suffering." It wasn't enough simply to forget the past. Joseph found the gold and became fruitful as well.

When putting the past behind you, discovering the treasure can soothe a wound better than any salve imaginable. The treasure may be increased knowledge of the character of God or a heightened awareness of Him working in your life. It could be a character trait of your own that is sharpened or spiritual growth that could only occur in the laboratory of life. The treasure might be a heightened sensitivity to the struggles of others. Like most treasure, you might have to dig through mounds of dirt before you discover it, but the eternal value is worth the effort.

An Only Son

Let me share with you one of my nuggets of gold. As you recall, my husband and I struggled for many years with secondary infertility after the birth of our son. We also lost a child due to a miscarriage. I loved being a mother, and my heart ached at the thought of not having a quiver full of children. I understood when I heard someone say that they never knew they could miss someone they had never met.

One night I stood in the doorway of my sleeping, then 17-year-old son's bedroom. He was six feet tall, with one hairy leg hanging out of the tangle of sheets. His face needed a shave, and his thick shock of hair was a tussled mop. *Lord,* I silently prayed. *I love this boy so much. Why were there no more children? Can you give me a nugget of gold today? I need a nugget of gold.*

Gently, the words of John 3:16 flooded over my entire being. *For God so loved the world that he gave his one and only Son, that whoever believes in him shall not perish but have eternal life.* I whispered the words and looked at my child. The words *only Son* resonated deep in my spirit. I had discovered the treasure.

I had an *only son,* and suddenly I had a glimpse of God's immeasurable love for me. There are many people I love a great deal, but there is no one for whom I would sacrifice my *only son.* And yet, God gave His only Son—for me. If for no other reason, I praise God for allowing me to understand more fully the magnitude of His sacrifice and the fathomless love He has for me—to give His only Son. Steven was a living visual reminder of God's love set before me.

I found the gold.

The Rose of Sharon

There have been other nuggets of gold forged from our experience with infertility. I discovered one while reading Song of Solomon 2:1. While reading the words of the groom to the bride, which I read as Jesus speaking to me—His bride—the words "I am a rose of Sharon" leapt from the page. I felt God speak to my spirit… *What is your name?*

My name is Sharon, Lord.

Look it up.

I pulled out a Bible dictionary and looked up the word "Sharon." It was a lush fertile valley in the Holy Land. Then the nugget of gold came to the surface.

My medical chart has the word *infertile* stamped on it, but my name, which I believe God ordained, means "fertile valley." Life may not have turned out the way I thought it would, with a house full of children with my blood coursing through their veins, but God did make my dream come true. Because of ministry, books, speaking, and radio, I am able to have spiritual children all around the globe! My book *Dreams of a Woman: God's Plans for Fulfilling Your Dreams* was born out of that struggle and that extraordinary moment with God.

Paul wrote, "No eye has seen, no ear has heard, no mind has conceived what God has prepared for those who love him" (1 Corinthians 2:9). When we give our broken dreams to God, He fashions them into a beautiful mosaic that is lovelier than anything we could have ever imagined.

A Purifying Fire

God uses trials and struggles to conform us to the image of Christ, shape our character, or remove impurities. When my husband was in dental school, he learned how to melt down gold to make crowns for posterior teeth. He heated the metal and removed the dross that rose to the surface. I asked him, "Steve, what exactly is dross?"

He very professionally explained, "It is the yucky stuff that makes the gold impure."

"Yucky stuff." I like that explanation. God removes the "yucky stuff."

When a goldsmith melts down a nugget of gold, dross or impurities rise to the surface. As the impurities are skimmed off the top, the gold takes on a brilliant luster. The goldsmith knows he is nearing completion when he can see his reflection in the liquid. The luster is a result of the light reflecting off of its pure surface—and that's what makes it beautiful. Satan wants to keep stirring up the impurities, but God wants to skim them off the top.

Job was a man who experienced a deluge of adversity. He suffered the loss of his children, his livestock (livelihood), and his health. In Job 23:10 he stated, "But he [God] knows the way that I take; when he has tested me, I will come forth as gold." Job knew the end product of his trials would be "gold."

God allows trials in our lives, and He uses them to remove the dross that blocks the reflection of His character in our lives. Change is rarely comfortable. Sometimes God has to turn up the heat. But the end product can be 100 percent gold bullion.

"All of us have had the veil removed so that we can be mirrors that brightly reflect the glory of the Lord. And as the spirit of the Lord works within us, we become more and more like him and reflect his glory even more" (2 Corinthians 3:18 NLT).

As my country grandmother used to say, "You're just gettin' purdier and purdier all the time."

Forgive Those Who Hurt You

C.S. Lewis said, "Everyone says forgiveness is a lovely idea until they have something to forgive."[1] Perhaps the most difficult facet of forgetting the past is forgiving those who have hurt you. But forgiveness is more about what you do than what was done to you.

Unforgiveness is a net and a snare. It will trap you like a spider that catches a fly in her web, and it will suck the very life from your soul. Paul warns us of this trap. "If you forgive anyone, I also forgive him. And what I have forgiven—if there was anything to forgive— I have forgiven in the sight of Christ for your sake, in order that Satan might not outwit us. For we are not unaware of his schemes" (2 Corinthians 2:10-11). The New American Standard Version states, "For we are not ignorant of his schemes." He warns us that unforgiveness causes a root of bitterness to spring up (Hebrews 12:15). Henry and Richard Blackaby explain it well:

> Bitterness has a tenacious way of taking root deep within the soul and resisting all efforts to weed it out…Time, rather than diminishing the hurt, only seems to sharpen the pain…You find yourself rehearsing the offense over and over again, each time driving the root of bitterness deeper within your soul…Bitterness is easy to justify. You can get so used to a bitter heart that you are even comfortable with it, but it will destroy you. Only God is fully aware of its destructive potential.[2]

Malcolm Smith gives this analogy:

> We find some perverse joy in licking old wounds. We return to the hurts again and again, reliving them in a movie we play in the theater of our minds…a movie in which we are the stars. We see ourselves abused, wronged—but oh so right. Every time we play this movie in our imagination we bear again what each person said or didn't say, what was done and how it was done. We cling to our memories because in our darkened minds we believe that if we forget,

the one who hurt us may go free!…Bitterness arises from the belief that the person who hurt us owes us and must somehow pay us back.[3]

Amazingly, many times the person we are holding a grudge against isn't even aware of it or doesn't care about the ill feelings. Ultimately, the only person being hurt is the person refusing to forgive. In essence, when we don't forgive, it is as though we are trying to punish the person by banging our own heads against the wall and saying, "Here, take that!" As I mentioned before, perhaps the person doesn't *deserve* to be forgiven. Perhaps you don't want to let the offender off the hook. None of us deserves to be forgiven, but look at how God forgave you and me. If we got what we deserved, we would all be sentenced to eternity in hell. But God gives us grace (receiving what we don't deserve) and mercy (not receiving what we do deserve).

When we let someone off of our hook and place him or her on God's hook, we will be free. It doesn't mean what the person did was not wrong. It does mean that you are no longer going to let the memory of it hold you captive. It means that you are no longer going to use the person's sin against him or her.

How much do we forgive? How many times? Is there any offense that warrants unforgiveness?

In Matthew 18:21-25, Peter asked Jesus, "Lord, how often shall my brother sin against me and I forgive him? Up to seven times?"

Jesus said to him, "I do not say to you, up to seven times, but up to seventy times seven" (NASB).

Sometimes I think I like Peter's ideas better—seven strikes and you're out, buddy. But Jesus is essentially telling us to put no limit on forgiveness. He even gives us a story to drive the point home:

> The kingdom of heaven is like a king who wanted to settle accounts with his servants. As he began the settlement, a man who owed him ten thousand talents was brought to him. Since he was not able to pay, the master ordered that he and his wife and his children and all that he had be sold

to repay the debt. The servant fell on his knees before him. "Be patient with me," he begged, "and I will pay back everything." The servant's master took pity on him, canceled the debt and let him go.

But when that servant went out, he found one of his fellow servants who owed him a hundred denarii. He grabbed him and began to choke him. "Pay back what you owe me!" he demanded. His fellow servant fell to his knees and begged him, "Be patient with me, and I will pay you back." But he refused. Instead, he went off and had the man thrown into prison until he could pay the debt. When the other servants saw what had happened, they were greatly distressed and went and told their master everything that had happened.

Then the master called the servant in. "You wicked servant," he said, "I canceled all that debt of yours because you begged me to. Shouldn't you have had mercy on your fellow servant just as I had on you?" In anger his master turned him over to the jailers to be tortured, until he should pay back all he owed.

This is how my heavenly Father will treat each of you unless you forgive your brother from your heart (Matthews 18:23-35).

The first servant was forgiven a debt that would amount to millions of dollars by today's standards, and yet he refused to forgive a debt that would be equivalent to just a few bills. I am the wicked servant. God is the king. He has forgiven me of so much. How can I not forgive others?

God's forgiveness should stir such love in us that we would long to forgive others in return. In Luke 7:36-50, a prostitute came to Jesus while He dined with a Pharisee. She wept, washed His feet with her tears, dried them with her hair, and anointed them with perfume. She was overcome with Christ's love and forgiveness. When the Pharisees questioned her acts, Jesus reminded them, "He who has been forgiven little loves little" (verse 47). She had been forgiven much—and as a result, loved much.

Back to our friend Joseph. Chuck Swindoll notes, "Joseph blazes a new trail through a jungle of mistreatment, false accusations, undeserved punishment, and gross misunderstanding. He exemplifies forgiveness, freedom from bitterness, and an unbelievable positive attitude toward those who had done him harm. He forgave those who had harmed him and made sure bitterness never had a chance to take root."[4]

Are you harboring unforgiveness in your heart? Remember the word picture I drew of the boys preparing to run the race with heavy backpacks strapped on their backs? Remember the word picture in Scripture of unforgiveness being someone strapped to your back—strapping the very thing you hate the most to your very being? Is there someone strapped to your back? Most likely some of us have an entire busload of folks tied on there. No wonder we find the "great race of life" tiring and cumbersome. God never intended us to run with such a load.

If you have someone strapped on your back, nothing in this book, no spiritual beauty treatment available, can erase the marring effects of unforgiveness on your soul. As I write, every time I type the word "unforgiveness" my spell checker underlines it in red to show that it is not a word. That's what Satan would have us believe. He would have us believe that unforgiveness is not a word and unforgiveness is not a problem. Believe me, unforgiveness is very real, and if left unattended, it can destroy your life.

Perhaps you are unsure if you have unforgiveness in your heart. Perhaps the unforgiveness has been there so long, it feels at home—as though it belongs there. "We cannot drop chains we don't even know we are carrying."[5] Stop and pray Psalm 139:23-24, "Search me, O God and know my heart; test me and know my anxious thoughts. See if there is any offensive way in me, and lead me in the way everlasting." Let me share how that prayer changed my life.

Cutting Dad Loose

After my sophomore year in college, I decided to take a break and work for a year or so. After the first year, I felt God was calling me to return to school, but it seemed an invisible force was holding me back. Plans were not falling into place, I was confused about where to go, and I could not get clear direction or peace from the Lord. Not to decide is to decide, so I stayed at my job another year.

When the second spring came around, my desire to return to school resurfaced. The confusion about what to do and where to go resurfaced as well. At the same time, I began having flashbacks of forgotten childhood memories.

I went to visit Mr. Thorp, a man who had been a spiritual mentor to me during my teenage years. I told him about my confusion about college and about the flashbacks. Mr. Thorp decided that we should read some Scripture about prayer before we prayed together for God's direction.

First he turned to Matthew 6:8-15:

> Your Father knows what you need before you ask him. This, then, is how you should pray: "Our Father in heaven, hallowed be your name, your kingdom come, your will be done on earth as it is in heaven. Give us today our daily bread. Forgive us our debts, as we also have forgiven our debtors. And lead us not into temptation, but deliver us from the evil one." For if you forgive men when they sin against you, your heavenly Father will also forgive you. But if you do not forgive men their sins, your Father will not forgive your sins.

Then he turned to Matthew 18:19:-22 and read Peter's question and Jesus' answer about how many times we need to forgive. In fact, each time Mr. Thorp turned to a passage about God answering prayer, there was one about forgiveness embracing it either before or after.

"Sharon," he said, "I sense that God is telling you that you have unforgiveness toward your father. Is that true?"

I wanted to say, "Wait a minute. I came here to ask for prayer about my future, not about my past." But God was showing me that unforgiveness in my past was blocking His work in my future.

At this time in my life, I had been a Christian for seven years. My father had become a Christian just a year before. I did not realize that I had not forgiven him for the pain he had caused in my childhood. When he made a mistake, all those old feelings I had toward him resurfaced. I knew now God was telling me that in order for my life to move forward in the future, I had to forgive the past.

That night I forgave my father for everything he had ever done. When I did, God set me free, and my life moved to a new and deeper level with Him. Interestingly, the next day, the cloud of confusion lifted. I applied to college in late spring, even though the head of the department told me it was too late and the program I desired to enroll in was full. They told me the only way I could get in was if someone were to drop out—which was very unlikely. Confident that this was God's plan for me, I resigned from my job and looked for an apartment near the college campus. Ten days before the start of the fall semester, the head of the department called and said, "This never happens, but someone just dropped out. We'd like you to come in the fall if you can make the arrangements."

I could believe it, and the arrangements were already made. I enrolled in the fall and met Steve four weeks later. Nine months after that, I became his wife.

I am not saying that when you offer forgiveness, you'll strike it rich, find the man of your dreams, or live happily ever after. However, I do believe that unforgiveness can block God's power in our lives and cause us to miss out on a storehouse of blessings.

I was in bondage for many years because of unforgiveness. Hear me here. It was bondage. I was held captive. But as Beth Moore states, "I never knew I was in bondage until Jesus began to set me free."[6]

In counseling sessions, Dr. Neil Anderson asks patients to make a list of those who have offended them. Ninety-six percent put father and mother as number one and two.[7] I did not realize how easy it was to be in that one or two position until I had a child of my own. Yes, my parents made mistakes. I, as Steven's parent, have made mistakes. Steven, when he becomes a parent, will make mistakes. It is not about the mistakes...it is about what we choose to do with them. The only perfect parent is our heavenly Father.

Now let's take a look at one more person we need to forgive... ourselves.

Forgive Yourself

Author David Seamands said, "There is no forgiveness from God unless you freely forgive your brother from your heart. And I wonder if we have been too narrow in thinking that 'brother' only applies to someone else. What if YOU are the brother or sister who needs to be forgiven, and you need to forgive yourself?"[8] Sometimes the hardest person to forgive is the person staring back at you in the mirror each morning.

The apostle John wrote, "If we confess our sins, he is faithful and just and will forgive us our sins and purify us from all unrighteousness" (1 John 1:9). God promises to forgive us our sins, and Satan promises to reminds us of our sins in order to prevent us from feeling forgiven. Who are you going to believe?

All God requires in order for us to receive forgiveness is repentance. Repentance is agreeing with God about your sins and turning to go in the opposite direction. However, repentance and forgiveness do not always remove the consequences of our sin. God forgave David for adultery and murder, but his firstborn son still died as a result (2 Samuel 12:13-18). Abraham was wrong to sleep with Hagar instead of waiting on God to provide a son through his wife, Sarah. God forgave Abraham, but as a result the descendants of Isaac (the Jews) and the descendants of Ishmael (the Arabs) are at war even today. He forgives sexual sin today, but unplanned pregnancies, sexually transmitted diseases, and alienated family members may be consequences that are the natural outgrowth of such choices.

F.B. Meyer wrote:

> Learn to forget...and do not dwell upon past sin. There may

be things in our past of which we are ashamed, which might
haunt us, which might cut the sinews of our strength. But if
we have handed them over to God in confession and faith,
He has put them away and forgotten them. Forget them,
and…the sin which has vitiated and blackened your record,
[and] reach forward to realize the beauty of Jesus.[9]

When Joseph's brothers came to the governor of Egypt for grain
during a time of famine, only to discover the governor was the
brother they had sold into slavery, I am sure they were filled with
guilt and remorse. But Joseph encouraged them to forgive themselves by saying, "Do not be distressed and do not be angry with
yourselves for selling me here, because it was to save lives that God
sent me ahead of you" (Genesis 45:5). Interestingly, the brothers
were brought back to Joseph after their initial visit because Joseph
had hidden a treasure in their saddlebags. When they came back to
the governor, he exchanged that hidden treasure for a much more
valuable one—forgiveness.

When I was a counselor at a Crisis Pregnancy Center, there was
a woman who came in because of depression she felt every spring.
During a session, she confessed that she had had an abortion on
April 5 at 10:30 AM more than ten years ago. Susan was now a
Christian, and she had asked God to forgive her, but she had failed
to forgive herself. She left Satan holding the trump card, and he
played it every spring. Through counseling in God's Word, she was
finally able to forgive herself and be free from her past.

Several years ago I learned an organizational tool for cleaning out
a closet. I place unwanted items in one of three bags: a put away bag,
a throw away bag, or a giveaway bag. I have learned that it is very
important to use bags I cannot see through! Why? You're smiling,
I can tell. Because we have a tendency to go back through the bags
and pull things back out. Sitting by the trash, suddenly, that old
belt doesn't look so bad anymore. And what was I thinking when I
put that sweater in the giveaway bag?

Friend, forgive yourself, and for goodness' sake, don't go back through the trash. You don't want it, God has already disposed of it, and it's not worth having.

A Woman Who Put the Past Behind Her

Cary was a woman who experienced a dramatic makeover once she learned the steps to leaving the past behind. Let me share her story with you.

Cary lived with her father, mother, and two older brothers in a simple bungalow with concrete floors, no running water, and an outhouse in the backyard. While her father was a cold, violent man, her mother was very loving and kind. Her earliest memory is when she was three years old. Her parents had a violent argument in which her dad punched a gaping hole in the den wall and then screeched out of the driveway in his car, abandoning the family. When Cary was four years old, her father returned, beat up her mother, and ripped her children out of her arms. He forced the crying children into his car.

"You can't take care of these children," he yelled. "You can't even drive a car. I've got a new wife who'll look after them better than you can. I'm taking them, and there's nothing you can do about it."

Cary's mother believed him and didn't try to get them back. Cary remembers peering out the rear window and seeing her mother's battered face standing in the doorway crying, "At least leave me my baby girl." Cary's heart broke as her father drove out of the driveway and away from her world. Cary's new stepmother was a cold, hard woman who showed little to no affection to her husband's three children. The trio lived for the weekends when they could visit their mother.

Shortly after Cary arrived at her father's home, he began sexually abusing her. Confused and afraid, she didn't know how to say no or that she even could. Before going to bed, Cary began wearing two to three pairs of pajamas and even using safety pins to hold them together. Still, her father violated her time and time again.

Cary's brothers missed their mother terribly. She had gotten married again to a violent alcoholic, and they constantly worried about her safety. At night, when their father and stepmother went out to dinner or to a movie, the boys called their mother's next-door neighbor. Their mother didn't have a telephone, so the neighbors ran next door to get her so she could talk to her children. One night, the call brought some news that shattered their world forever.

"Hi, this is Allen and Bobby. Can you go get my mom?" "I'm sorry, boys. Didn't someone tell you? Your mom's husband shot her in the back today and then killed himself. Your mother's dead."

The one person who loved Cary the most was gone forever.

The sexual abuse continued. When Cary was 14 years old, she gathered up enough courage to lock her door. The next day, her enraged father took the door off its hinges, and Cary lost all privacy or protection.

When she was 16 years old, her father was in a car accident that caused him to be home during the day. Summer was approaching, and Cary was terrified of what he would do to her on the long summer days. Finally, she gathered the courage to tell the authorities. They promised they would come and get her, but they never did. In desperation, she called the school guidance counselor and begged him to rescue her from this 12-year nightmare. The counselor did come, but because he did not know where to take her, he took her to a juvenile detention center. The center was filled with girls who were being punished and one girl who was being protected—Cary.

The weeks Cary spent at the detention center were the most secure two months of her young life. Bars keeping the girls in and Cary safe. One Sunday, a Baptist preacher came to the detention center and presented the gospel of Jesus Christ. At last, Cary heard that someone loved her. At the close of the service, he asked, "If anyone would like to accept Jesus as their personal Savior, please stand." With tears streaming down her cheeks, Cary stood.

Three weeks after Cary's arrival at the center, an aunt who lived on the West Coast came and took her to live with her and her husband. Eventually, they adopted her as their own child. Cary believed that she now had a chance to see what a real family was like. That dream was quickly shattered.

Cary adored her uncle and trusted him with all her heart. However, he destroyed that trust when he made sexual advances toward her two years after her arrival. Once again, a father figure violated her. Only this time, Cary knew she could have said no, but didn't. She felt dirty, ashamed, and worthless. Cary went off to college, and like the woman at the well, tried to fill her emptiness the only way she knew how: with men. She married at 18, but had it annulled 6 months later. She married again at 20, but divorced after 6 years. She married again at 26, and divorced after 14 years. She married again at 40, but divorced 3 years later.

One night, she met Jesus at the well of His Word. She opened up her Bible in search of verses on joy. *Surely the Bible can tell me how to find real joy,* she thought.

She turned to Psalm 16:11: "You will fill me with joy in your presence." Then to Romans 4:7-8, "Blessed are they whose transgressions are forgiven, whose sins are covered. Blessed is the man whose sin the Lord will never count against him." She flipped to John 15:11-12, "I have told you this so that my joy may be in you and that your joy may be complete. My command is this: Love each other as I have loved you." Then to 1 John 1:9: "If we confess our sins, he is faithful and just and will forgive us our sins and purify us from all unrighteousness."

The Holy Spirit opened her eyes to the truth that would set her free.

"God, are You telling me that in order to find happiness, I must forgive?"

One by one, Cary began to pray and forgive those who had hurt her. "Lord, I forgive my father for abusing me. I forgive my stepmother for not protecting me. I forgive Jake for killing my mother. I forgive Uncle James for seducing me." With each person Cary forgave, she felt a release as if the shackles of oppression were dropping from her arms, legs, and heart. There was only one person she did not forgive that night, but it was a start.

When I met Cary at a women's retreat, she listened intently as I spoke about running the race like Paul. "We must forget the past: the good that we've done, the bad that others have done to us, and the ugly that was done through us," she heard me say. "We must find the hidden treasure, forgive those who have hurt us, and forgive ourselves."

There was one person Cary had not forgiven—herself. She had made a series of bad choices throughout her life, and Satan reminded her of them daily, but finally, on a Saturday in March 2000, Cary decided to stop listening to the voice of the accuser and believe the truth in 1 John 1:9. That day, Cary forgave herself and was finally free.

Today, Cary is running the great race of life unencumbered. And like the woman at the well, she has left her water pot and brought an entire community to the Man who told her about the living water that quenches so we will never thirst again. Today she is a speaker and Bible teacher who shares God's freeing truths with all who will listen. She has found the gold by using her past experiences to lead them to the One who sets the captive free.

Your Invitation to Freedom

North Carolina has birthed some very influential men and women. Perhaps one of our favorites is Andy Griffith of the *Andy Griffith Show*. In Andy's fictional town of Mayberry lived a town drunk named Otis. When Otis was arrested for public drunkenness, Andy put him a jail cell until he sobered up. After a good night's sleep, Otis would wake up, simply stick his hand through the bars of the jail cell door, take the key from a nail hanging on the wall, and let himself out. It was just that simple. On a few occasions, Otis stumbled into the jailhouse and locked himself in the cell, placing the key back on the nail on the wall.

This was always a comical scene, but it reminds me of the jail we lock ourselves in when we remain a prisoner to our pasts. Our key to freedom isn't hanging by a nail on a jailhouse wall, but hung by a nail on a rugged cross. His name is Jesus.

The key is within reach. Will you be free?

A Brand-New Wardrobe
Replacing Rags with a Royal Robe

Her daddy called her his "little princess"—not just because she looked like one, but because she actually was one. Tara's daddy was the king, and she was indeed his little princess. Her name meant "palm tree," a symbol of victory and honor. But as we all know, being born into a wealthy, prestigious family does not ensure a peaceful, happy life void of heartache, tragedy, and despair. Thus was the case for Tara.

Tara had several siblings: brothers, half brothers, sisters, and half sisters. It was a royal blended mess. One half brother in particular made her feel very uncomfortable. Aaron stood too close to her when he spoke, held her a bit too long when they greeted one another with a hug, and complimented her with a gleam in his eye that did not seem quite brotherly. On many occasions at the dinner table, she felt his eyes burning a hole right through her. When she dared to meet his gaze, he smiled a toothy wicked grin that sent chills down her spine. Being in his presence made her feel as though she had walked through a spider web and left her trying to wipe away an invisible netting that clung to her soul.

One day Tara mentioned her uneasiness to her sister.

"Oh, that is just his flirtatious personality," her sister chided. "Besides, what makes you think he would be interested in you? It's only your imagination, silly girl."

Tara was not imagining her half brother's infatuation. Aaron lusted after Tara both day and night with impure thoughts and desires. His passionate longings were so consuming that a friend noticed his frustration.

"What's wrong with you, Aaron?" his friend asked. "Why do you look so haggard morning after morning?"

"I can't get any sleep," Aaron answered. "All I can think about is getting Tara into my bed."

The friend's pulse quickened at the mere mention of Tara. She was indeed beautiful in form and face.

"You are a prince, aren't you? Here's what you need to do…" and the two of them devised an evil plan.

The next day Aaron pretended to be sick. When his father came to check on him, he said, "Dad, I don't feel well, and the only food that sounds good to me is some of Tara's sweet rolls. Would you please ask her to bring some to my room?"

At her father's request, Tara brought Aaron a plate of freshly baked bread still warm from the oven. But it was not the delicious aroma of Tara's cooking that caused Aaron's senses to stir. When she approached his bed, he quickly commanded all the servants to leave the room and lock the door behind them. The young girl dropped the plate and froze in fear. Aaron grabbed his sister and threw her across his satin sheets. She wrestled, fought, and pounded on her half brother's chest and face and arms, but the struggle only seemed to make him more aggressive and passionate. She was no match for his strength and determination. In less than ten minutes, Tara lost her most precious possession, her virginity.

After Aaron's obsession had been satisfied, he pushed his sister onto the floor in disgust. Now he hated her more than he had ever loved her.

Tara fled from Aaron's bedroom with tears streaming down her cheeks and blood trickling from the corner of her mouth. She tore off the royal robe of a virgin princess and wailed through the castle halls looking for her best friend, her brother Alexander. Alexander heard her cries, ran to meet her with a fatherly embrace, and swore to get even.

"Shh," he said, holding his index finger to his lips. "Don't tell anyone this has happened. Come and live at my house for a while."

Tara was inconsolable and spent the rest of her days in darkened desolation and isolation at Alexander's home. She never again put on the royal robes of a princess, but wore only sackcloth with ashes heaped upon her head.

This story reads as though it came from the pages of the *National Inquirer,* from a made-for-TV movie, or an afternoon soap opera. While I have embellished the details, the story is from 2 Samuel 13 in the Bible and tells the sordid drama of three of King David's children. Tara is Tamar, Aaron is Amnon, and Alexander is Absalom.

Tamar's story may be your story. If you have ever been sexually or emotionally abused, you have something in common with Tamar. If you have ever been shamed or rejected, you have something in common with Tamar. If something despicable has ever happened to you and others advised you to keep quiet, you have something in common with Tamar. If you have ever felt unprotected by your earthly father, you have something in common with Tamar. If you have lived in mourning and desolation, you have something in common with Tamar. But no matter what your particular situation may be, there is one thing you do *not* have in common with Tamar. Tamar's father left her in sackcloth and ashes and didn't do anything to restore her to her rightful position as a princess. Your heavenly Father made a supreme sacrifice to give you a new wardrobe and place you back in the royal court.

The Original Wardrobe

When I was ten years old, my grandmother started me on a journey of becoming a seamstress. Our first project together was to transform a rectangular piece of fabric into a nicely gathered apron with two front pockets and an ample sash that tied around my tiny waist. How significant, for the first article of clothing young Eve crafted in the Garden of Eden was an apron as well.

Let's go back to the Garden and peek into Eve's sewing room.

In chapter 3 we saw how Satan tempted Eve to disobey God's one command and eat from the tree of the knowledge of good and evil. When Eve and Adam disobeyed God and ate the fruit, their eyes were opened. They saw their nakedness and ushered in two new emotions: fear and shame. In an effort to cover their shame, Eve devised a needle and thread of sorts and sewed fig leaves together to make "aprons" (Genesis 3:7 KJV). Other translations of the Bible call them "coverings" (NIV) or "loin coverings" (NASB). But the best translation is "aprons." The Eve original just covered front and center—only the part she could see.

Just as Eve tried to camouflage her shame with an apron, we still tend to try to cover our shame with modern day aprons. But there's one thing about an apron—especially if it is the only thing you're wearing. An apron doesn't cover your backside. I'm sure as soon as Adam and Eve turned to walk away Satan snickered at the sight.

Have you ever made an apron to cover your shame? Maybe not a literal apron, but some other type of modern day fig leaves? Women don't even wear aprons much these days. But perhaps we try to cover our shame with beautiful clothes, a perfectly decorated home, or personal achievements.

The only time I've ever worn a real apron is when I'm working. Have you ever tried to cover your shame by "working for the Lord"? Have you ever tried to earn your acceptance or pay penance by your service? If we are hiding behind an apron, we might fool some of the people some of the time, but sooner or later we're going to have to walk away—and look out for what's exposed!

God saw Adam and Eve's pitiful aprons (and their backsides) and knew their feeble attempt at covering their shame was insufficient. So He killed an animal, made garments of skin and clothed them— front and back. This was the first recorded blood sacrifice and a foreshadowing of the sacrifice that was to come. While this covering provided a temporary covering of their shame, God devised another plan to cover man's shame once and for all. He provided another sacrifice, His only Son, Jesus Christ. Because of Jesus' death on the cross and resurrection from the dead, our sins have been covered by His blood. When we accept Jesus as our Savior, one of the benefits of becoming a child of God is receiving a new wardrobe. We are clothed with Christ's righteousness. We are clothed with Christ Himself (Galatians 3:27).

A beautiful word picture of being clothed with Christ is found in the book of Judges. When God called the cowardly Gideon to become the leader of the Israelite army, the Bible says, "Then the Spirit of the LORD came upon Gideon" (Judges 6:34). The Hebrew word for "came upon" is *labesh,* which means "wrap around, put on a garment or clothes."[1] The Interlinear Bible notes it this way: "The Spirit of Jehovah clothed Gideon with Himself." Isn't that a wonderful picture of God wrapping Gideon in Himself? Can you imagine? You should, because you have also been clothed with Christ in the same way. It's a perfect fit, designed by God.

One of the results of the exercise program (running with the goal in mind) and the weight loss program (leaving the past behind) is the need for a new wardrobe. For those who have had a dramatic weight loss, you know the excitement of having to purchase new clothes to fit your new look! In the ultimate makeover, God has purchased a new wardrobe for you, and He's waiting to place it on your shoulders.

David sang, "You have removed my sackcloth and clothed me with joy" (Psalm 30:11). Isaiah rejoiced, "He has clothed me with garments of salvation and arrayed me in a robe of righteousness" (Isaiah 61:10). Jesus' disciples were clothed with power from on high (Luke 24:49). And Paul wrote to the Galatians, "All of you who were baptized into Christ have clothed yourselves with Christ" (Galatians 3:27). No more are we clothed in the sackcloth of shame, dear friend, but in the righteousness of Christ.

Back to Tamar

Through my work in ministry to women, I meet many who suffer needlessly just like Tamar. They may not be walking around with ashes on their heads or dressed in burlap sacks, but they wear the mantle of shame that Satan has placed on their shoulders and secured with deception. They may have children, a husband, a successful career, and look beautiful on the outside, but many are spending their days in desolation of the soul because Satan has convinced them that's where they deserve to stay. Wearing the cloak of shame because of past abuse, misuse, or mistakes, they don't realize that Jesus Christ has purchased a robe of righteousness for them and He's eager to place it on their shoulders. Perhaps you are one of those women who needs to change her wardrobe.

Let's go back to Tamar for a moment. Let's pretend the story didn't end as it did in 2 Samuel. Imagine with me, if you will…

Tamar had lived in desolation and isolation for many years. Her body was frail from lack of appetite, nourishment, and exercise. Her arms and legs were calloused and raw because of the never-ending rubbing of the burlap over her once-smooth skin. The ashes had worked their way into her pores so that she had the ashen-gray appearance of death. No one in her brother's household had been able to console Tamar. After a while, they simply tired of trying.

One day she was awakened from her trance as her bedroom door creaked open, and a stream of light burst into the room. Standing in the doorframe was the figure of a man she did not recognize but yet seemed familiar. The light followed Him as He approached her as if it was emanating from His body instead of some outside source. He was dressed in a shimmering white robe and looked like the Son of God. She dared not meet His gaze, but hung her head in the shame that had become her signature cloak.

"Do not be afraid, My precious one," He spoke softly. "My Father, the King of heaven and earth, has sent Me to you."

Tamar could not bear to raise her eyes to meet His, so He placed His hand under her chin and gently lifted her head. Their eyes locked, and she felt warmness run over her chilled body. With His thumb He wiped away a tear that trickled down her cheek and cupped her face in His hands. Such love and compassion she had never known.

After what seemed like an eternity, He held out His hand and Tamar fit hers into His palm. When she did, she noticed a scar in the palm of His hand the size of a nail and her name engraved directly under it. Without saying a word, He dipped a cloth into His side and washed her with His blood. Beginning at her head and ending at her toes, the years of soot and filth began to disappear and Tamar's skin shone white and pure as a newborn babe. Not only was her skin clean and pure, but her sackcloth had been transformed into a royal robe more beautiful than the ones she had worn in her father's court.

He looked deeply into Tamar's eyes and whispered, "I have come to bind up the brokenhearted, to proclaim freedom for the captives and release from darkness for the prisoners. To comfort all who mourn, and provide for those who grieve, to bestow on them a crown of beauty instead of ashes, the oil of gladness instead of mourning and a garment of praise instead of a spirit of despair." *

Tamar had never felt freer in all her life. No more shame. No more despair. Suddenly she began to sing a song she had heard her father play on his harp many years ago: "You removed my sackcloth and clothed me with joy" (Psalm 30:11). "I delight greatly in the Lord, my soul rejoices in my God. For He has clothed me with garments of salvation and arrayed me in a robe of righteousness" (Isaiah 61:10).

Jesus countered her with His own song of promise. "Those who look to him are radiant; their faces are never covered with shame" (Psalm 34:5).

It was then that they danced.

Dear sister, when your heavenly Father looks at you, He sees you clothed in Jesus Christ—pure, holy, and spotless. Don't let Satan convince you to put back on the sackcloth of shame. God has provided a new wardrobe and we need never wear those old hand-me-downs again!

---

* See Isaiah 61:1-3.

Slough Off the Old

Getting Rid of Old Habits
and Thought Patterns

Of all the activities ten-year-old Miriam enjoyed, she loved riding horses the most. Charlie, her favorite horse, had a sleek chestnut mane, well-defined muscular legs, and a fierce strong will to match. Miriam felt powerful and self-assured when controlling this massive animal—except, that is, when he caught a glimpse of the barn. Whenever Miriam and Charlie returned from a jaunt in the woods, as soon as they got close enough for him to see the barn, he bolted homeward, forcing Miriam to hang on to the reins for dear life.

One day, Miriam's riding instructor witnessed this strong-willed animal taking control of his master. She was indignant.

"Miriam! What are you doing?" she called out. "You cannot let that animal control you in that manner! Bring that horse back out of the barn this instant."

Dutifully, Miriam mounted Charlie and rode him a distance away from the stalls.

"Now," the wiser, older woman instructed, "when you turn around and Charlie sees the barn and begins to run toward it, turn your reins all the way to the right. Do not let him go forward."

On cue, Miriam steered her horse toward the stalls. On cue, he began to bolt.

"Turn him! Turn him!" the instructor shouted.

Young Miriam pulled the reins to the right as hard as she could until the horse's head was inches away from touching his right shoulder. But instead of obeying her lead, Charlie fought her with the force of a war horse. Round and round the horse and rider circled.

"Don't let go," the instructor shouted. "You must break his will!"

After ten long minutes of going in circles, Miriam and Charlie grew exhausted and quite dizzy. He stopped circling. She stopped pulling him to the right.

"Now gently tap him to see if he will walk toward the barn instead of run," the instructor commanded.

Charlie did not bolt, but walked at a steady pace. Miriam had broken the horse's will, and she now regained control of this beautiful animal as he submitted to his master's touch.

Changing the Way We Act

When I took piano lessons, I quickly became frustrated. I didn't want to learn how to play the piano; I wanted to play the piano! Many times when learning a new skill we don't want to practice; we want immediate results. When the results don't come instantly, we become frustrated and give up.

Everything mentioned in the previous pages moves us to the desired result of changing the way we act. If we put the cart before the horse and start out trying to change our actions without changing our hearts and minds, we will become frustrated. That is what the Pharisees did. It is called legalism and does not lead to freedom in Christ or inner beauty. We've learned the truth. Now let's apply it to our actions.

Just as Miriam's horse had a tendency to bolt toward the barn because that was the pattern he had developed after many years, we tend to fall back into engrained habit patterns learned during those formative years of trying to get our needs met independently from God. Unfortunately, when we become a Christian no one pushes the delete button on those old ways of acting and thinking that have been programmed into our minds. Exfoliating the old way of living in the flesh begins when we renew our minds with the truth of God and continues when we apply that truth and walk in the Spirit. We must give the reins of our lives to Jesus and yield to our Master's control. But I have to warn you; sometimes you might find yourself going in circles as the Master tries to break your stubborn will.

Paul was no stranger to this struggle of changing the way we act. In Romans 7, he lets us have a peek into his own personal battle:

> I do not understand what I do. For what I want to do I do not do, but what I hate I do. And if I do what I do not want to do, I agree that the law is good. As it is, it is no longer I myself who do it, but it is sin living in me. I know that nothing good lives in me, that is, in my sinful nature. For I have the desire to do what is good, but I cannot carry it out. For what I do is not the good I want to do; no, the evil I do not want to do—this I keep on doing. Now if I do what I do not want to do, it is no longer I who do it, but it is sin living in me that does it. So I find this law at work: When I want to do good, evil is right there with me. For in my inner being I delight in God's law; but I see another law at work in the members of my body, waging war against the law of my mind and making me a prisoner of the law of sin at work within my members. What a wretched man I am! (verses 15-24).

Paul was in quite a predicament. He felt wretched. I've been there right along with him. Have you? As long as we depend on our old flesh patterns and old way of doing things, dear sisters, we will feel wretched most of the time. Paul knew in his mind what he wanted to do, but his body, like Miriam's strong-willed steed, wanted to do the opposite. Theologians for centuries have argued whether Paul was writing about his life before or after his conversion. I can see arguments for both sides. While that may remain unclear, one thing is certain—in these verses Paul was a man trying to "do good" in his own strength.

Here's an exercise for you. Go back and reread those verses, marking each time Paul uses the words "I," "my," or "me." How many do you count?

Paul uses more than 30 personal pronouns when describing his struggle to make his walk match his talk. That's a lot of "me, myself, and I"! Therein lies the problem. When we focus on our own strengths and abilities, apart from Christ, we will always come up lacking. We live in a culture that says, "Pull yourself up by your own bootstraps." "If you can dream it, you can achieve it." Avis Rent-a-Car used to boast, "We try harder." Unfortunately, "We try harder" is the banner flying over many of our churches and hearts today.

I have some startling news for you. Living the Christian life is not difficult. It is impossible, and the harder you try in your own strength, the more frustrated you'll become. Jesus is the only one who has ever lived the perfect Christian life, and He is the only one who can live it today. The good news is—He wants to live it through you!

But how? Paul knew the problem, and he also knew the solution. He was so excited to tell us the answer, he couldn't even wait until Romans 8, but blurted it out at the end of Romans 7: "Who will rescue me from this body of death? Thanks be to God—through Jesus Christ our Lord!" (Romans 7:24-25). Jesus said, "You will know the truth, and the truth will set you free" (John 8:32). He also said, "I am the way and the truth and the life" (John 14:6). It is only when we know Jesus, the truth, that we can be set free from the legalistic bondage of trying to live the Christian life in our own strength.

As Paul discovered, trying harder is not the answer. Letting Jesus live through us is. In Galatians 2:20 Paul said, "I have been crucified with Christ, and I no longer live, but Christ lives in me. The life I live in the body, I live by faith in the Son of God, who loved me and gave himself for me." We can never experience freedom walking in the flesh—depending on our own abilities apart from Christ. We only experience freedom walking in the Spirit and identifying with the death, burial, and resurrection of Jesus Christ.

Breaking the Power of the Flesh

Paul wrote, "Those who belong to Christ have crucified the

sinful nature with its passions and desires" (Galatians 5:24). If that is the case, then why do we continue to struggle with the flesh in our daily walk? Neil Anderson explains: "It is important to recognize that our crucifixion of the flesh is not the same as the crucifixion of the 'old man' or 'old self' (Romans 6:6)." The old man was crucified by God when we came to Christ. That is a finished work. Anderson goes on to say, "The flesh is no longer the dominant controlling characteristic of our lives…The characteristics of the old man are still present, albeit no longer representing our true identity."[1] We crucify the flesh daily by the decisions we make. However, the power to make those decisions must come from the Holy Spirit. We can't do it on our own.

Breaking the cycle of living in the flesh is done through the power of the Holy Sprit, but we have to participate with Him. He gives us the power; we plug into the power source and make a decision to put to death the desires of the flesh. Did you catch that? It begins with a decision…in the mind.

The Bible teaches that our struggles and temptation come from the world, the flesh, and the devil (Ephesians 2:2-3). The world can be defined as "the whole system of humanity (its institutions, structures, values, and mores) as organized without God."[2] The world promotes self-sufficiency. The flesh is our old way of living apart from Christ. And, of course, we are all too familiar with the devil. It is virtually impossible to tell if temptation is a result of the world, the flesh, or the devil because they are so intricately intertwined. The world constantly seeks to pull us away from God by appealing to our flesh. At the same time, John says, "We know…that the whole world is under the control of the evil one" (1 John 5:19). The three are partners.

But even these three enemies cannot come close to matching the power that is at work within us! "This is the victory that has overcome the world, even our faith. Who is it that overcomes the world? Only he who believes that Jesus is the Son of God" (1 John 5:4-5). "The one who is in you [Jesus] is greater than the one who is in the world [Satan]" (1 John 4:4).

God assures us that we will never be tempted beyond what we can endure and will always provide a way of escape (1 Corinthians 10:13). We can never say "the devil made me do it" because he didn't. He may have made the suggestion, but we make the decision. Like a contestant on a game show, we stand before door number 1 and door number 2. Behind door number 1, marked "Walk in the Flesh," hides temporary pleasure that leads to death. Behind door number 2, marked "Walk in the Spirit," hides eternal victory that leads to life.

Walking in the Spirit

In a factory where delicate fabrics were woven, the machine operators were told to call on the supervisor should the thread at any time become entangled in the equipment. One woman had worked at the factory for many years and knew the machines well. When her threads became entangled in the gears, she tried and tried to pull them out.

After several minutes, she had created a disastrous mess, putting the expensive machine in jeopardy.

Finally, she called the supervisor and defended herself by saying, "I did my best!"

The supervisor answered, "No, you didn't. To do your best would have been to call on me."

We can try our best to fix ourselves, but actually doing our best is calling on God, depending on Him, and walking in the Spirit. Paul wrote, "Walk by the Spirit, and you will not carry out the desire of the flesh. For the flesh sets its desire against the Spirit, and the Spirit against the flesh; for these are in opposition to one another" (Galatians 5:16-17 NASB). There is a continual battle going on between the flesh and the Spirit, or the old way of doing things apart from Christ and the new way of doing things in union with Christ. It is a choice we make every moment. But praise God, He has given us everything we need to live a life of godliness and the truth. We simply make the choice to partake.

What does life led by the Spirit look like? Paul paints the stark contrast of life controlled by flesh (living in our own strength) in Romans 7 with the life lived controlled by the Spirit (depending on God's strength) in Romans 8. The verses in Roman 8 are a balm to the Christian. Here are just a few:

- Therefore, there is now no condemnation for those who are in Christ Jesus (verse 1).

- You received the Spirit of sonship. And by Him we cry Abba, Father (verse 15).

- We are God's children (verse 16).

- We are heirs—heirs of God and co-heirs with Christ (verse 17).

- I consider that our present sufferings are not worth comparing with the glory that will be revealed in us (verse 18).

- We know that in all things God works for the good of those who love him, who have been called according to his purpose (verse 28).

- In all things we are more than conquerors through him who loved us (verse 37).

- [Nothing] will be able to separate us from the love of God (verse 39).

In Romans 7, when Paul focused on "me, myself, and I," he was pitiful. In Romans 8, when Paul focused on life in the Spirit, he was powerful. It is the result of sanctification: "The process of becoming in your behavior what you already are in your identity. Your old self is dead, but the flesh and sin live on, battling your new self daily for control of your life. Spiritual growth and maturity result when you believe the truth about who you are and then do what you are supposed to do to renew your mind and walk in the Spirit."[3]

The world, the flesh, and the devil hinder walking in the Spirit.

All three work together to tempt us to have our God-given needs met in things, circumstances, and people rather than in Jesus Christ. We defeat the flesh every time we make a decision to follow Christ rather than our old sinful, selfish ways of doing things. We defeat the world every time we choose to believe the Bible rather than the culture that promotes values and perspectives that are totally opposite from God's. We defeat the devil every time we choose to believe the truth rather than his lies.

Walking in the Spirit is characterized by the fruit of the Spirit: love, joy, peace, patience, kindness, goodness, faithfulness, gentleness and self-control (Galatians 5:22-23). Oh, how I wish I could reduce life in the Spirit to a formula to follow, but I cannot. Life in the Spirit is the supernatural result of maturing in a personal and ongoing relationship with Jesus Christ. The more intimately we know and obey Him, the more we will become conformed to His image and the more beautiful we will become.

Walking in the Spirit is a consistent moving forward toward the cross. It is not accomplished by filling up your days with endless activities or service. As Jesus told Martha, Mary's busy sister, "My dear Martha, you are upset over all these details! There is really only one thing worth being concerned about. Mary has discovered it—and I won't take it away from her" (Luke 10:41-42 NLT). "Satan knows that he may not be able to stop you from serving God by making you immoral, but he can probably slow you down by simply making you busy."[4]

Jesus invites us to learn how to walk by being yoked to Him. He said, "Take my yoke upon you and learn from me" (Matthew 11:29). In Jesus' time, when a farmer trained a young ox to plow, he yoked the youngster to a more mature ox. The younger ox did not actually pull any weight, but simply walked alongside his "teacher." Likewise, Jesus invites us to walk alongside Him. He will carry the heavy load; we simply keep pace with Him.

Pitiful Patty or Powerful Paula

We can all agree that we need to live our lives in the Spirit (being controlled by the Holy Spirit and depending on His power within us) and not in the flesh (living life in our own strength and power), but we don't always recognize the flesh when we see it. That is largely because some people's flesh looks better than others.

Let's take Pitiful Patty and Powerful Paula. Pitiful Patty is always depressed, sees herself a victim of circumstance, and tries to get her needs met by acting pitiful and whiney. Nothing ever works out for the poor girl. She's learned that if she acts pitiful, people will feel sorry for her and not expect much from her, because she's...well, pitiful, bless her heart.

Then there's Powerful Paula. She takes charge, could run IBM single-handedly, and exudes confidence and courage. Powerful Paula gets her needs met by performing well in order to hear those wonderful words "well done" and "good job." She thrives on the praises of others. People expect a lot from Paula, because she's...well, powerful.

As a Christian, Pitiful Patty has an easy time believing 2 Corinthians 12:9: "My strength is made perfect in weakness" (KJV), because she is in tune with her weakness. Paula, on the other hand, resonates with "I can do everything through him who gives me strength" (Philippians 4:13), because she's been doing it on her own all her life anyway.

The truth is, both women are operating in the flesh if they are continuing in old habit patterns engrained after years of practice.

Are you a Pitiful Patty or a Powerful Paula? Most of us fall somewhere in between. I have to admit, however, that most of my life I've tried to make myself look like Powerful Paula while feeling more like Pitiful Patty.

Amazingly, two different children raised in the same household with the same stimuli can form two different flesh patterns or ways of dealing with life. For example, let's take two siblings, Becky and Jonathan. They grew up in a home where their parents fought continually. Their father was an alcoholic and their mother was a controller. With this volatile combination, they witnessed many explosive outbursts.

In an attempt to protect their emotions, the two children

responded in different ways. Many nights Becky stood between the two parents, literally breaking up the fights. She became a "fix-it person." On the other hand, her brother fled the scene and became an "exit person." At first he got on his bike and pedaled away. Then, when he grew older, he grabbed the car keys and drove away.

The two children grew up to be adults with very ingrained patterns of handling stress. Becky continued to be a "fix-it person." She tried to fix everybody and everything. Jonathan continued to be an "exit person," leaving every time life became difficult. He quit the football team in high school when someone questioned his ability. He quit college when the course load became too strenuous. He quit his marriage when he and his wife encountered financial difficulties. He quit ten jobs in ten years because his bosses "were unfair."

While Becky's unique version of the flesh looks better on the outside, it is still flesh nonetheless. Neither will find true peace and happiness until they learn to walk by the Spirit.

Perhaps being a controller (fix-it person) or a quitter (an exit person) is not a flesh pattern that you can relate to, but any coping mechanism that is separate from Christ is operating in the flesh.

How do you begin to walk in the Spirit? You begin just as a baby learns to walk—one step at a time.

> *Sow a thought, reap an action.*
> *Sow an action, reap a habit.*
> *Sow a habit, reap a lifestyle.*

Victorious days lead to victorious lives. If I were to write another book titled *How to Live the Victorious Christian Life,* it would have two words on every page...Follow Jesus. That's it. Immerse yourself in Him.

Learning How to Walk

When my son was four years old, we decided it was time to take the training wheels off his little red bicycle. With a mixture of fear and excitement, Steven mounted the seat with my hand on the back fender to help keep him steady. He placed his feet on the pedals and wobbily made his way across the lawn. I ran alongside him to keep him from falling. After a few trial runs, it was time for me to let go. When he noticed that I was no longer running beside him, Steven panicked and tumbled to the ground.

"I can't do it," he cried.

"Sure you can," I cheered. "Once you get the hang of it, riding your bike will be the *funnest* thing you do as a kid. Let's try again."

For about 30 minutes Steven attempted to steady the bicycle on his own. Finally, he threw the bike to the ground, stood with his hands on his hips, and announced in frustration, "I can't do it. This is not fun, and it will never be fun!"

We put the bike away.

You can guess what happened. Several days later, once the frustration had abated, Steven mounted the bike and tried again. This time his body worked in tandem with the bike, and he mastered his steed. The following weekend, when we went to visit my mother, he insisted that we pack his bicycle. For hours he pedaled around her cul-de-sac...it was the *funnest* thing he had ever done.

Walking in the Spirit and changing old habit patterns and ways of thinking aren't as easy as learning how to ride a bike, but they do take practice. At first we may fall and skin our knees, wobble instead of walk, and battle with frustration. But when we fall, we simply get back on and try again.

There is a good reason this chapter is at the end of the book. We tend to want a magic formula or ten steps to success (or thinner thighs in ten minutes a day). However, understanding the truths in the previous pages makes this chapter possible. Without changing the way we think, we cannot change the way we act.

Also, we must remember that changing the way we act does not happen overnight. Like an amputee who reaches to scratch his missing leg, we may have lingering remembrances of the life we've left behind. Does a recovering alcoholic never again long for the warm brown liquid to course down her throat and sting her senses? Does the previously promiscuous woman never ponder the thrill of seduction? Does the silenced gossiper never crave the sensation of owning the power of hidden secrets? I don't know if the desires of the flesh are ever cast off for good, but I do know that the more we practice righteousness and obey the Master's leading in our lives, the *less* we fall into the ruts of the old life and the *more* we walk in newness of life in sync with God.

A Day at the Spa

Spending Time with the One
Who Makes You Beautiful

I was comfortably snuggled in a warm black leather reclining chair which vibrated at calibrated intervals up and down my body. The room was dimly lit with clusters of flickering scented candles. My mind relaxed as stringed instruments wafted through the air like invisible winged fairies, and the sound of ocean waves crashing on the shore washed over me. Ahhhh, this was definitely one of my husband's best gifts ever...a day at the spa.

I really didn't know what to expect when I walked through the doors to redeem my gift certificate, but I was pleasantly surprised. Betty first dipped my hands into melted paraffin and then placed my wax-coated skin into warmed mittens. She then led me into the candlelit room, seated me in an overstuffed recliner, and told me to relax. She returned after a few moments and exfoliated, massaged, and moisturized my face and scalp. Reluctantly, I sat up and placed my feet in a warm bubbly massaging tub. My feet floated on air after the 45-minute pulsating bubble bath, calf massage, and pedicure.

Next, my hair was submitted to the beautician's comb and brush for a trendy new look. A white tipped-French manicure made my 40-something hands look young and vibrant. The makeup artist applied the proper colors in all the right places, and I left feeling like a queen.

A day at the spa! What a delightful treat! But that was on a Friday, and by Monday the visit seemed like a distant memory. The dry flakes returned to my face, the tension knots reappeared in my neck, the red polish had chipped around my twin big toes, bathroom cleaner with bleach had caused my white French manicure to turn a pale shade of yellow, and my hair refused to submit to my commands—exchanging the trendy new look for early American housewife frump.

Yes, every woman loves the idea of spending a day being pampered from head to toe—but the results are temporary and oh so fleeting. However, there is one spa where the results are lasting, the doors are always open, and the Beauty Artist is always awaiting our arrival. And the best part is the price has already been paid. Each and every one of God's children has a standing appointment with God to be refreshed, renewed, and revived today and every day—to be made beautiful with glowing, lasting results.

Everything I've written on the previous pages hinges on one pivotal point. In order to experience the ultimate beauty treatment, we must spend time with the Beauty Artist—God. Being conformed to the image of Christ doesn't happen when we merely acquire more head knowledge, memorize more Bible verses, or master Greek and Hebrew derivations and verb tenses. Being a reflection of His glory is a direct result of spending time in His presence, embraced in His love, and enveloped in His grace. Moving from one state of glory to the next does not occur by following a list of rules. It is a supernatural result of developing an intimate ongoing, ever-growing relationship with Jesus Christ. The outward, visible signs of such a relationship occur when we give Jesus total access to our lives so He can inhabit every nook and cranny of our minds, wills, and emotions to live His life through us. When He does, our walk will be in tandem with His.

In the New Testament, the Pharisees were the religious experts of their day. They had a lot of head knowledge about God but little to no heart relationship with Him. They knew about God, but they did not know Him personally.

In the Old Testament, the Israelites were satisfied knowing about God, but they never desired to know Him personally. They witnessed miracles He performed and ate food He provided, but they remained content partaking of His provisions without ever knowing the Provider. They even requested that God not speak to them directly, but only through His messenger (Exodus 20:19).

But Moses was a man who knew God on a personal level. God even referred to Moses as His friend (Exodus 33:11). One defining characteristic of Moses was his frequent trips to God's spa—extended periods of time spent in God's presence. One particular visit lasted for 40 days and 40 nights (Exodus 24:18). When he came down from Mount Sinai, he was radiant—his face actually shone. Moses' visits with God had such glowing results, he had to place a veil over his face so the glory would not blind those who looked at him. In between his times with the Lord, the glorious glow gradually ebbed away (2 Corinthians 3:13). But each time he spent time in the Lord's presence, he was reenergized and the intensity of the glow returned.

Have you ever had a mountaintop experience at a women's conference, spiritual retreat, or extended time alone with God? You returned home with a smile on your face, a song in your heart, and a bounce in your step. But after a few days, your husband said something that made the hair stand up on the back of your neck, your teenager broke curfew again, and your neighbor called to complain that your dog dug up her prize rosebush. (I've often said I could be a great Christian if it weren't for people.) It doesn't take much of life to give us a bad case of the *uglies*.

So how do we maintain that holy glow in our hearts amid the struggles of daily life? We visit God's spa for the soul on a regular basis. When we do, 2 Corinthians 3:18 becomes a reality in our lives. "We, who with unveiled faces all reflect the Lord's glory, are being transformed into His likeness with ever-increasing glory, which comes from the Lord, who is the Spirit."

Have you ever noticed how married couples begin to look alike, speak alike, and move with mirrored mannerisms? Have you observed lifelong friends use similar words, copy figures of speech, and dovetail ideas? After Jesus' arrest, some bystanders recognized

Peter as one of Jesus' followers. One of them said, "The way you talk gives you away" (Matthew 26:73). Peter talked like Jesus and didn't even realize it.

Likewise, when we spend time with God, we will begin to talk like Him, think like Him, and respond to life like Him. Who do you want to be like? Do you want to be like the women you are watching on TV or do you want to be like Jesus Christ? You will become like the company you keep.

A Standing Appointment

I usually visit my hairdresser every six to eight weeks for a trim. However, she has a rather large clientele of older ladies who come once a week—every week. Barbara calls these her "standing" appointments. Unless Claire is on vacation or in the hospital, she has a standing appointment at 10:00 every Tuesday morning. Louise is in the chair every Monday at noon, followed by Mabel at 1:00. Each week, Barbara shampoos, curls, cuts, colors (if needed) coiffures, and spraaaaays their hair. On the days in between, the ladies simply pick, fluff, and reapply spray to keep their sculptured hair intact until their next visit. Mayhem breaks loose when Barbara takes a vacation, as panic-stricken women scurry about for temporary solutions!

My husband was shocked when I explained this weekly ritual that his own mother had participated in for decades. He couldn't fathom washing his hair only once a week, but I explained churchgoers do it all the time. They go to church on Sunday for their weekly cleansing and sprucing up, and then never give God another thought until the following week.

But God has an appointment book with "standing" appointments for each us—not once a week, but every day. He is waiting to cleanse us and beautify our souls every morning. To help you remember the importance of this rendezvous with God, I've come up with the simple acrostic DATE. Keeping a DATE with God on a regular basis is the only way to experience the ultimate makeover with lasting results.

D—Determine to Spend Time with God

I have two identical jars in my workroom. One is three-fourths full of sand. The other contains fist-sized rocks. The jar of sand represents my activities on any given day: to-do lists, grocery shopping, community projects, housecleaning, etc. The list is as endless as grains of sand. The other jar containing the large rocks represents what God wants me to do on any given day: spend time with Him, study His Word, and pray—my daily beauty treatment.

If I fill the jar with large rocks first, amazingly, I can pour all the sand from the other jar into it and the sand fits in nicely around the nooks and crannies. However, if I begin by filling the jar with sand and then try to squeeze the rocks into the same jar, they won't fit.

Likewise, if I start my day spending time with God (the rocks), everything else (the sand) seems to fall into place. If I spring out of bed and hit the floor running to tackle all the tasks that I feel are so necessary for the day first, somehow my time with God just never seems to fit in.

I keep these two jars in my workroom as a reminder to keep my priorities in order and begin my days with the large rocks. This is not a legalistic self-imposed mandate. It is a privilege to have an audience before the King of kings. The jars are there to help remind me that He's waiting for me to show up.

Jesus said to Martha, "My dear Martha, you are so upset over all these details! There is really only one thing worth being concerned about. Mary has discovered it—and I won't take it away from her" (Luke 10:41-42 NLT). Mary started her day with the big rocks. Undoubtedly, Martha started hers with sand. The Bible never tells us what Martha and Mary look like, but in my mind's eye, I've always envisioned Martha as harsh and stern-faced and Mary as tenderly beautiful. I don't know why. All we're told is one spent time at Jesus' feet and the other spent time in the kitchen. Come to think about it—that's all the reason in the world.

A—Appoint a Specific Time Each Day

Let's face it. We are creatures of habit. If we can establish a specific time to meet with God each day, we will be more likely to show up for our appointment. When Jesus taught His disciples to pray, He said, "Give us this day our daily bread." David and Nehemiah both sought the Lord "day and night," not just when they were in need. God provided manna for the Israelites every morning (except on the Sabbath). When a few Israelites tried to gather extra food so they wouldn't have to gather God's provisions the next day, they found their bowls full of worms the next morning. God wants us to seek Him for our daily—not weekly or biannual—bread.

Some tell me that they have their quiet time on the way to work, in the carpool line, or on their lunch break. This seems to me like going into a five-star restaurant, ordering a multicourse meal, and asking the waiter to put it in a to-go bag.

My best time to visit God's spa is in the morning before the tyranny of the urgent begins to pull me in various directions. When I spend time in the morning, God helps me order my days and keep His perspective on what is happening around me.

In Mark 1:35 we see that Jesus also began His days communing with the Father. "In the early morning, while it was still dark, Jesus got up, left the house, and went away to a secluded place, and was praying there" (NASB). Interestingly, in the next verse, Mark describes a scene where the disciples were looking for Jesus. It seems that the people in the town where Jesus had been the day before were pleading for Him to return and heal more people. The disciples said, "Everyone is looking for You." And He replied, "Let us go somewhere else to the towns nearby, so that I may preach there also; for that is what I came out for" (verse 37-38 NASB).

Jesus had met with the Father and received His marching orders for the day. He was able to say yes and no with confidence because He knew what His Father had planned for Him to do on that particular day. Would going back to Capernaum and healing more people have been a good thing to do? Yes, it would have been good, but it wasn't God's best. It wasn't what God had planned for Jesus on that day. He knew how to prioritize the good for the goal.

I don't know about you, but by 8:30 in the morning my phone

is ringing with all kinds of requests and demands on my time. By spending time with God first thing, I'm able to set my priorities for the day and say yes and no with confidence. In my book *A Woman's Secret to a Balanced Life,* I mentioned this idea of having a DATE with God each day. I was very reluctant to say that the DATE should be in the morning. I understand the struggles of a mother with a new baby, the woman who works the night shift, or the person who has to leave for a 5:30 AM commute to work.

Yes, it *is* more important *that* you have a quiet time with the Lord than *when* you actually have it. However, I'm going to let Bruce Wilkerson, author of *The Prayer of Jabez* and *Abiding in the Vine,* tell us his opinion:

> Some Christians I know try to have their meaningful personal times with God just before bed, but I have yet to find a respected spiritual leader throughout history who had devotions at night. Unless you get up early, you're unlikely to break through to a deeper relationship with God. Set aside a significant time and a private place where you can read and write comfortably, think, study, talk to God out loud and weep if you need to…To break through to abiding I must broaden my devoted time—taking it from a morning appointment to an all-day attentiveness to His presence.[1]

David wrote, "In the morning, O LORD, you hear my voice; in the morning I lay my requests before you and wait in expectation" (Psalm 5:3).

Studies show that it takes seven weeks of doing something routinely to form a habit. Appoint a specific time each day to spend with the Lord and stick to it for seven weeks. When you've established your standing appointment, you will be more likely to show up—and what an incredible life-changing habit you will have formed.

T—Take Time to Pray

When I decided to set up a standing appointment with God

each day, I wasn't sure exactly what I was supposed to do during that time, so I read to see what Jesus did. First and foremost, I noticed that Jesus spent His time in prayer.

During my ten years working at Proverbs 31 Ministries, my son always knew where to find me. One night he was looking for me, and the first place he called was my ministry partner's cell phone. He knew the chances were pretty great that I was either with Lysa or she would know where I was. Likewise, when Jesus' disciples were searching for Him in Mark 1:35, they knew where to look. He was off with the Father in prayer.

Some of the greatest moments in a Christian's life are a result of spending time in prayer. Jesus spent all night in prayer before He chose His disciples (Luke 6:12). He defeated Satan's temptations after praying and fasting for 40 days (Matthew 4:1-11). Prayer preceded His miracles (John 11:41-43) and gave Him the strength to go to the cross (Luke 22:39-43). Jesus showed us how to have more than a prayer life. He showed us how to have a praying life.

The disciples observed the power that came as Jesus spent time with God in prayer and asked Him to teach them how to pray. He gave them seven simple steps that we have come to know as "The Lord's Prayer" (Matthew 6:9-13 KJV):

1. *Our Father which art in heaven.* Acknowledge that you are a child of God and He is your almighty Father with whom you have a relationship.

2. *Hallowed be thy name.* Praise God for who He is and the holiness of His name and character.

3. *Thy kingdom come. Thy will be done in earth, as it is in heaven.* Pray for His will to be done in your life and the lives of those for whom you intercede. Praying the Word of God is praying the will of God.

4. *Give us this day our daily bread.* Pray daily for your needs.

5. *And forgive us our debts, as we forgive our debtors.* Confess your sins and ask God to forgive you. Also, forgive those who have offended you.

6. *And lead us not into temptation, but deliver us from evil.* Pray for protection from the world, the flesh, and the devil.

7. *For thine is the kingdom, and the power, and the glory, forever.* Praise God once again. He is the eternal King of kings whose rule knows no end. He is omnipotent, omniscient, and omnipresent. Amen.

In *Experiencing God,* Henry Blackaby writes, "Prayer is not a substitute for hard work. It is the work!"[2] Prayer isn't meant to change God's mind. It is meant to align our thinking with God's and change us with the power necessary to change the world.

Know this, dear sister, Satan knows that *prayerless* lives are *powerless* and *unprotected* lives. He will try to distract you in any way he can. When you sit down to pray, the phone may ring, ten things to add to your to-do lists may mysteriously pop into your mind, your eyelids may become heavy, and the demands and concerns of the day may press in to invade your time—but don't let the enemy win. Prayer is the makeover tool that turns concerns into comfort, chaos into calm, and cowards into conquerors. Keep your appointment in prayer. You'll be amazed how it can be the oil to make the wheels of the day turn smoothly.

E—Examine God's Word

If you ran out to your mailbox and retrieved four pieces of mail—a letter from Aunt Susie, a bill from the phone company, a department store flyer, and a letter from God, which one would you open first? I don't know about you, but I'd rip open that letter from God faster than a two-year-old tearing into a beautifully wrapped Christmas present! The truth is, God has sent us a wonderful love letter filled with treasures of encouragement, words of endearment, instructions for empowerment, and makeover tips to make us beautiful from the inside out. All we have to do is open up the pages of the Bible and engage.

Matthew Henry said prayer is a letter we send to God; the Bible is a letter God has sent to us. One way God communicates with us is through the words in the Bible.

Second Timothy 3:16-17 says, "All Scripture is inspired by God and profitable for teaching, for reproof, for correction, for training in righteousness; so that the man of God may be adequate, equipped for every good work" (NASB). When you read God's Word and hide it in your heart, you are equipping yourself for the days ahead. I love how 1 Peter 1:13 says, "*Gird* up the loins of your mind" (KJV). When I see the word "gird" I can't help but think of my grandmother's old-fashion girdle. It held her in, held her up, and she wouldn't leave home without it. Likewise, we shouldn't leave home without girding our minds for action.

When I am under stress, I tend to have three recurring dreams. In one, I'm in high school. It's the day of final exams, but I realize I haven't gone to that class all year. In my second dream, I'm working as a dental hygienist with one patient in the chair and five patients in the waiting room. I'm two hours behind and can't find my instruments. In my third dream, I'm standing behind a podium in a crowded room. I'm not dressed in a power suit but in my birthday suit. After some reflection, I realized that each of these nightmares is about not being equipped—not being prepared.

The Bible is designed to lead us to God and draw us into a closer walk with Him. As we walk close beside Him, we will experience His power in our lives. He performs a makeover and turns defeat, discouragement, despair, doubt, dread, and depression into love, joy, peace, patience, kindness, goodness, faithfulness, gentleness, and self-control. It is part of the great exchange.

In my book *Becoming a Woman Who Listens to God,* I give this analogy for approaching God's Word:

> One summer I went to Europe and visited many art museums. I recall strolling down the aisles of the Louvre in Paris, quickly glancing at first one masterpiece and then another. Finally, I decided to stop and look at one particular painting. I don't even remember which one it was. The more I looked at the painting, the more I began to see. It was dark on one side and grew lighter on the other. I noticed the expressions on the faces, the longing of a child,

the pain of a man, the approaching cloud in the sky, the hues of the clothes, a bare foot, a torn robe, a clenched fist. A story began to unfold before my eyes, and it was as if I were beginning to see into the heart of the artist.

This reminded me of how some read the Bible—as though they are perusing through an art gallery and never really stopping to see what the artist intended in the great masterpieces lining the majestic walls. Like walking briskly through an art gallery, we grab the Bible and read a few verses before running out the door in the morning or closing our eyes at night.

But God's Word is a masterpiece, and He speaks through every stroke of the writer's pen. Oh, the treasures stored on each page just waiting to be discovered![3]

A.W. Tozer once said:

> Every farmer knows the hunger of the wilderness. The hunger which no modern farm machinery, no improved agricultural methods can quite destroy no matter how well prepared the soil, how well kept the fences, how carefully painted the buildings, let the owner neglect for a while his prized and valued acres and they will revert again to the wilds and be swallowed by the jungle or wasteland. The bias of nature is toward the wilderness, never toward the fruitful field.[4]

If we desire to cultivate the fruit of the Spirit in our lives, we cannot leave our spiritual lives to chance but must nurture our relationship with Christ. By determining to have a time with God each day, appointing a specific time each day, taking time to pray, and examining God's Word, we will grow more beautiful each and every day.

Getting Started

If you are not in the habit of spending time with God each day,

I want to encourage you to start with realistic goals. Begin with spending five minutes a day—three minutes reading the Bible and two minutes praying. Then increase your time to fifteen minutes a day—eight minutes reading the Bible and seven minutes praying. If having a quiet time with the Lord each day is a new concept for you, deciding to set aside an hour each day may be inviting failure. Start slowly. Just as a person who has not been eating due to illness must start by eating small bits at a time, you may need to begin by ingesting small bits of the Word of God. Once you begin to feast on God's Word and bask in His presence, the benefits and beauty that follow will be all the enticement you need to visit God's spa often.

Perhaps you've tried many times to begin having quiet times with God each day, but have broken your appointments. Please don't become discouraged. Draw near to God and He will draw near to you (James 4:8 NASB). " 'Return to Me' declares the LORD Almighty, 'and I will return to you' " (Zechariah 1:3).

Dazzling Results

Putting the
Pieces Together

I had been speaking all morning at a ladies retreat in Virginia and welcomed the one-hour lunch break to rest my feet and my voice. Lisa, the women's ministry director, was very attentive and sat with me while I munched on salad and sipped sweet iced tea. She was a beautiful woman with stylish short blonde hair, a winning vibrant smile, and an effervescent personality that bubbled over with Jesus Christ. Her crisp blue suit accentuated the aquamarine of her eyes, and her matching shoes put the finishing touches on a woman who looked as though she had it all together. It was evident by the hugs and pats on the back that Lisa was the spiritual mentor and confidante to many women in the church.

I asked, "Lisa, what's your story? How did you come to Christ?"

I can tell you, there is no way I could have ever been prepared for what I heard over the next 30 minutes. Brace yourself and listen to her story.

"Sharon, I was born into a family with three older brothers. I don't remember much of my early years, but one of my earliest childhood memories is of me when I was five years old standing on a bridge and thinking, *If I fell over this rail into the river and disappeared, no one would ever care.* I always felt as though something was wrong with me—like I was a misfit or an irregular.

"I remember my mother saying to me, 'What's wrong with you?'

"As a little girl I thought, *I don't know, but I know it must be something!* I felt uncomfortable in my own skin, as though I didn't belong, wasn't accepted, lovable, or valuable.

"When I was 13, I took my first drink of wine. I actually downed three bottles in one sitting. It felt good. I felt good. All my insecurities were gone. I lost my virginity when I was 14 and smoked marijuana for the first time that same year. For the next 28 years, I chased after anything and everything to numb my pain. Whether it was food, exercise, shopping, men, alcohol, or drugs—I sought after anything that would transport me into a different world for a while and fill the gaping void in my soul.

"After high school, I worked in Washington, DC, at a law firm. But that didn't last very long as I was fired for falsifying records. After that, I went to work as a bartender. My alcohol and drug use began to escalate, and I began to plummet. I moved in with a man who beat me up on a regular basis. I felt I deserved it.

"One night I reached the end of my rope and tried to kill myself with sleeping pills. For some reason I called my mom to say goodbye, and she alerted the rescue squad. Even though I spent time in the psychiatric ward, I left the hospital just as lost and confused and desperate as when the ambulance had brought me in.

"Cocaine is very expensive, and I needed a way to support my habit, so I became a prostitute on the streets of Washington, DC. With every trick, a piece of me died. Pretty soon, I became numb to it all. Amazingly, I was arrested for writing bad checks, not prostitution. My attorney got me out of jail and into a recovery program. This was the beginning of a long road to recovery, but the reason I am alive today is because I met someone. It wasn't a lawyer, a mentor, or the man of my dreams. His name is Jesus Christ, and He's the one who set me free."

I sat there with a lump in my throat, tears in my eyes, and love for my Savior pounding in my heart. I had asked a simple question. "Tell me your story." Never had I had such a filling delicious lunch in all my life.

What exactly happened to Lisa? How did God transform an

alcoholic cocaine-addict prostitute into a pure, holy, lovely Christian woman who is so filled with the Holy Spirit that He seeps out and spills on to everyone she comes in contact with? Lisa met the Beauty Artist and experienced the ultimate beauty treatment. She would be the first to tell you it has been a long, arduous process, but the refiner's fire has produced a beautiful woman both inside and out.

That's what the ultimate beauty treatment is all about: death to life, darkness to light, dejection to love.

A Priceless Jewel

To celebrate our twenty-fifth wedding anniversary, Steve and I took a land and sea excursion to Alaska. The landscape was captivating as we traveled from the snowcapped mountains of Mount McKinley, through the majestic masses of ice at Glacier Bay, to the wildflower-covered tundra of the Interior.

Larry and Cynthia Price, our good friends from college days, took the journey with us…which was actually the best part of the trip. The first part of the excursion was on land, and the second was by sea. While on the cruise ship, we docked at various Alaskan fishing villages to mill around the shops and get a taste of Alaskan civilian life. When the boat docked at Juneau, it seemed that everyone had lost their steam for wanderlust and opted to stay on the ship for the morning. But not me. I put on my jeans, donned my tennis shoes, and grabbed a credit card and ID. Off I traipsed to explore the shops and do what I do best…look for bargains.

I think I'll look into buying a tanzanite stone to go on my gold necklace, I thought to myself. *Everyone seems to be talking about the beautiful tanzanite here.*

I spotted a store with a banner that beckoned me with bright red letters. "End of the year closeout!" If I'm anything, I'm thrifty, so I decided this was the store for me.

I waltzed into Diamonds International with one purpose in mind—get a good deal. Right away I felt a bit out of place in my tennis shoes and jeans. The pristine showroom with crystal chandeliers, sophisticated suit-clad sales associates, and sparkling glass cases lined with jewels didn't give the impression of a discount or closeout store, but the sign had said…

"May I be of assistance?" Gretchen asked. A sleek saleswoman with a European accent gracefully swept her manicured hand across the glass case. "Are you looking for something in particular?"

"Yes," I answered. "I'm looking for a tanzanite slide for my necklace."

"Right this way," she answered as she elegantly glided across the room.

"Oh, I like this one," I said right away. "How much is it?"

"It retails for 83, but our closeout price is 43."

Suddenly, I remembered that I had a coupon for this store back on the ship, but I couldn't remember the details of the discount. "I have a coupon back on the ship. Should I go back and get it?"

"That won't be necessary," she replied. "We will honor it." Then she pulled out her calculator, began punching in numbers, and then lowered the price.

"Is it a special occasion, such as a birthday or anniversary?" she asked.

"Yes, it is our twenty-fifth anniversary."

"Even better. We can give you an even better price."

I was getting excited as the price continued to drop! Then the store manager came over to the case.

"Hello, ma'am," he said. "Have you been looking at this stone for quite some time?"

"Oh, no," I responded. "I just saw it a few minutes ago and decided I liked it."

"I'll tell you what," he continued. "I'll give you this tanzanite for 27 if you promise to wear it to dinner tonight and tell everyone where you got it and what a great deal you got."

"That sounds like a great deal," I said. "Let's do it."

So I pulled my credit card from my jeans pocket and the stone was mine. As Gretchen rang up the purchase, the store owner filled out an appraisal. I thought it was a bit strange to fill out an appraisal for such a small amount, but hey, what did I know? I got my purchase, stuffed it in my sweatshirt pouch and headed out to peruse a few of the other jewelry stores.

I think I'll buy some earrings to match, I thought. As I went from store to store, I realized what a good deal I got at Diamonds International, so I decided to go back for another purchase. The wheeling and dealing followed the same pattern as before. They told me the suggested retail, then their closeout price, then the lower price because I was so special to them. Bottom line? Twenty-two. Sounded good to me.

We followed the same process. I gave the salesperson my credit card and the manager began filling the appraisal. But one small difference was that I looked at the receipt before I signed it.

"Oh, I'm sorry, miss. You've made a mistake," I said when she handed me the receipt. "This says the charge is 22 *hundred* dollars instead of 22 dollars."

"That is correct," she said.

"No, you said 22," I said with a voice that had suddenly jumped two octaves. "You never said the word *hundred!*"

"Oh no, mademoiselle. The earrings are 22 *hundred* dollars."

I dropped the receipt as though it had suddenly burst into flames. "I don't want them. There has been a big misunderstanding!" Then a sinking feeling hit as I put my hand in my sweatshirt pouch and felt my previous purchase.

"What did I just buy an hour ago?" I asked as I pulled the stone from my pouch.

"That was 27 *hundred* dollars," she clarified.

"I thought it was 27 dollars!" I shrieked. "You never said the word hundred! Not once!"

Thankfully, they took back the stone I had purchased and credited my account. I ran back to the ship as fast as my little tennis shoes could carry me and promised to never go shopping without an escort again! (At least not in Alaska.) Can you imagine if I had come home, opened my credit card bill and seen a 49-hundred-dollar charge rather than a 49-dollar charge? Oh, my. Steve affectionately calls that the day I went into Juneau, Alaska, and proceeded to spend our son's inheritance.

When we got home, I told Steven the story. He didn't laugh like everyone else. He just looked at me dumbfounded and said, "Mom, didn't you pick up on the clues?"

"Like what?"

"Like, you were in DIAMONDS International. The stone was in 14 KARAT GOLD. It had little DIAMONDS around it."

"Yeah, but they were very little diamonds!"

"The manager wrote out an APPRAISAL. He wouldn't do that for 27 dollars."

"But it was an end-of-the-season closeout sale …"

Steven just looked at me and shook his head.

You know, he was right! All along, there were hints that the tanzanite was much more valuable than 27 dollars, and yet I refused to pay attention to the clues.

Oh, dear one, you are of great value to God. Have you been paying attention to the clues? You are His treasured possession. There is no closeout sale, end-of-the-year clearance, or discount coupon when it comes to your worth as a child of God. All through our lives, God gives us clues about our worth. The beauty of a sunset, the soothing sound of a baby's coo, the sweetness of a fresh strawberry, the warmth of a hug, the comfort of a phone call, the answer to a prayer, the sacrifice of His Son. God loves and values you so much, He allowed and purposed for His only Son, whom He loved, to die on a rugged Roman cross to pay the penalty for your sin so that you could spend eternity with Him. He didn't have to do that, you know. But He did it because of your great worth to Him.

Here is another hint or clue of your value to Him…this book. I believe that the reason you are reading this book is because God is giving you yet another hint of His great love for you and your worth to Him. He has given you a new identity. You are redeemed, restored, and renewed. Bought with a price…all sales final…no returns.

Putting the Pieces Together

By nature I am a very organized person. Most days run smoothly. My files are color coded, my spices are alphabetized, and I've only lost my car keys twice in my life. Someone approached me about writing a book on organization to help women find order among chaos, but in truth, I don't really know what I do. It is just the way I came out of the womb. I probably began organizing the doctor's surgical instruments and straightening his face mask moments after he cut the cord and popped me on the bottom.

We tend to learn through the struggles and trials of life and not through what comes easily. I can assure you that is how I learned about experiencing the ultimate makeover—through the refiner's fire. I have lived every page of this book. Let me take you back to where we began in chapter 1, to the little girl who was held captive by feelings of inferiority, insecurity, and inadequacy.

"From the time I was 14 until I was in my early thirties, I always felt as though something was wrong with me spiritually—as though I had walked into a movie 20 minutes late and had to spend the entire time trying to figure out what was going on. I wondered why I struggled so to live the victorious Christian life. I had a wonderful husband, an amazing son, and a happy home life. I taught Bible studies at a scripturally solid church, and I surrounded myself with strong Christian friends. But something was missing—I didn't know who I was. I did not understand the change that happened in me the moment I became a Christian. I didn't understand my true identity as a child of God."

One day I picked up a book by Dr. Neil Anderson, *Victory over the Darkness,* and read a list of who I was in Christ. At that moment my thirst for understanding this truth began. For ten years I spent many hours in God's spa learning what the Bible said about who I am, what I have, and where I am in Christ. I realized that the enemy had declared all-out war to keep me from becoming the woman God had intended, and I began to fight back with the sword of the Spirit...the Word of God. I went back to the enemy's camp and took back what he stole from me. No longer would I be that little girl in the first grade sitting in the caboose of the spelling train who thought she was stupid or that scared child who thought nobody loved her. They were lies—all lies. The Bible said that I had the mind of Christ and everything I needed for life and godliness and truth. I chose to believe it. It has been a tedious process to change the old way of thinking, but the Holy Spirit renews my mind each time I study God's Word.

I can write about having a confidence makeover because I've seen how God took an insecure girl like me and transformed her into someone who knows what God can do through a life totally yielded to Him. I can write about having a faith lift because I have seen the difference it makes when we believe God tells the truth. I can write about leaving the past behind because I've left much baggage by the roadside, never to return to pick it up again. I can write about a change of wardrobe because I sat for many years in desperation and shame with Tamar, but rejoiced when I finally accepted the mantle of a princess from my Redeemer. I can write about sloughing off old dead flesh patterns because I'm still in the process of scrubbing them off every day.

Dear sister, I long to be with you right now. This book is so much a part of my life. It isn't my first book, but without the message of the ultimate transformation, there would have never been any of the ones before it or the ones that will follow. How I have longed to grab your hand and take you to God's spa to experience the ultimate beauty treatment. Thank you for joining me. I can already sense the beauty of Christ illuminating from your face as you reflect His glory. You are beautiful, dear one. Absolutely radiant.

"All of us have had that veil removed so that we can be mirrors that brightly reflect the glory of the Lord. And as the Spirit of the Lord works within us, we become more and more like him and reflect his glory even more" (2 Corinthians 3:18 NLT).

Deep Cleansing

Bible Study

Lesson One—What's Your Story?

1. Everyone has a story. In this introductory lesson, consider telling or writing your story. If this is something you have never considered, answer the following questions. You may want to draw a timeline and mark key events of your life.

- Where and when were you born?

- Describe your family growing up.

- When was the first time you remember hearing about Jesus?

- Who was the most influential person in your spiritual awakening?

- When did you first believe that Jesus was the Son of God who died for your sins and rose again that you might have eternal life?

- How did that decision change your life?

- How have you grown in your relationship with Christ since that time?

- What have been times of greatest growth and times of greatest struggle? (These may very well be the same.)

- What is the state of your spiritual life today? (Example: growing, learning, thriving, struggling, questioning.)

2. No matter where we are on your spiritual journey, we are all in the process of the transformation. God will change us to the extent that we yield to Him. Read the following account of Jesus at the wedding party in Cana. (John 2:1-11)

    a. What was the dilemma at hand?

    b. What were Mary's instructions to the servants? (verse 5)

    c. What were Jesus' instructions to the servants? (verse 7)

    d. Suppose the servants had filled the jars halfway full. How much would Jesus have turned to wine?

    e. How much of your mind, will, and emotions do you desire Jesus to transform? Are you willing to experience a total transformation and be filled to the brim with Christ?

Lesson Two—It All Started in the Garden

1. Read Genesis 1:20–2:7 and note the difference between how God created animals and man. What made man unique?

2. Read Genesis 2:17 and note the penalty for eating of the tree of the knowledge of good and evil.

3. What does Ephesians 2:1 say about our state before we accept Christ?

4. Read Matthew 23:27-28. How is a spiritually dead person who acts "religious" like a *whitewashed tomb?*

5. How did sin enter the world? Through whom? (Romans 5:12-14)

6. How is spiritual life made available? Through whom? (Romans 5:15-19)

7. Just as sin entered the world in the Garden of Eden when man decided to disobey, where was the victory won when Jesus determined to obey? (Matthew 26:36-42)

8. What do these two verses tell you about why Jesus came? (John 10:10; 1 John 3:9). How have you seen His purpose fulfilled in your own life?

9. If you had been with Nicodemus the night Jesus told him "You must be born again," how would you have explained what Jesus meant? (John 3:3)

10. How did Paul see himself as a "born again" believer? (2 Corinthians 5:17)

11. Read and record what Jesus said about "life."

    a. John 1:14

    b. John 11:25 *eternal*

    c. 1 John 5:12 have to believe in Jesus

12. Jesus' work was finished on the cross, but the decision to obey occurred in the Garden of Gethsemane. Compare what happened in

the Garden of Eden and the Garden of Gethsemane. Which garden reflects your life? In which garden do you long to live?

— make the decision to obey

Lesson Three—Experiencing the Great Exchange

1. Read Ephesians 2:1-3 and list everything you learn about the state of a person before they accept Christ.

2. The book of Romans wonderfully outlines the spiritual makeover that happens when each person accepts Jesus Christ as Lord and Savior. Look up and record the following verses. Consider memorizing these verses.

   a. Romans 3:23-24

   b. Romans 5:8

   c. Romans 6:23

   d. Romans 8:1

   e. Romans 10:9-10

   f. Romans 10:13

3. Read 1 Corinthians 1:30 and describe how God sees us in Christ.

4. To whom is this righteousness made available? (Romans 3:22,26,30)

5. Let's look at some before and after pictures of the great exchange.

Before We Accept Christ	After We Accept Christ
Ephesians 2:1-3	Romans 6:11
Colossians 1:21	Galatians 3:26-29; 4:6-7
Ephesians 5:8	Ephesians 5:8
1 Corinthians 2:14	1 Corinthians 2:16

6. Can you describe your before Christ picture and your after Christ picture?

7. What does Satan attempt to do? (John 10:10; 2 Corinthians 4:4)

8. What does Jesus offer to anyone who believes? (John 3:16; John 10:10)

9. God has begun a good work in you! What does He promise to do with what He has begun? (Philippians 1:6; 1 Thessalonians 5:23-24)

Lesson Four—Your Beautiful Reflection

1. Now that you know who you are in Christ, let's look at a few more verses about what comes with our new identity.

   a. Ephesians 1:4

   b. Ephesians 1:7-8

   c. Ephesians 2:4-5

   d. Ephesians 2:18

   e. Ephesians 3:12

f. Colossians 1:14

g. Colossians 1:27

h. Colossians 2:7

i. Colossians 2:10

j. Colossians 2:12

k. Colossians 2:13

l. Colossians 3:1-4

2. Look at what Christ endured to make our new identity possible. Read the following verses.

a. Isaiah 53:1-12

b. 2 Corinthians 5:21

c. Hebrews 2:6-10

3. Read Isaiah 43:1-10 and answer the following.

a. According to Isaiah 43:10, why were we chosen by God?

b. What is the difference between "to know" and "to believe"?

c. How does God feel about you?

d. Why were you created?

4. Read 2 Corinthians 3 and note everything you learn about the word "glory."

5. If you could describe what glory looks like, what do you see? Use your imagination. There is no right or wrong answer here.

6. What did Jesus show us while He was here on earth? (Hebrews 1:3)

7. What do we show the world by our lives?

8. What does Paul call Christians in 2 Corinthians 3:2? Who is reading you?

Lesson Five—Contagious Courage and Christ-Powered Confidence

1. Read Exodus 3:10–4:14. Make two columns on your paper. In one column note Moses' objections to God's call on his life and in the other note God's response to those fears or objections.

2. Read Joshua 1:5-9.

   a. What was God's commission to Joshua?

   b. What were God's specific promises to Joshua?

3. Thought question: Why did Noah continue building the ark even though he had never seen rain and the townspeople made fun of him? How does this relate to confidence? What was the result of his obedience?

4. Where does fear originate? (2 Timothy 1:7)

5. One of the seeds of fear is when we begin to depend on our own

abilities. Read 2 Corinthians 1:9 and note what Paul said was the purpose of struggles.

6. Read the following and note what you learn about depending on our own abilities and talents instead of Christ in us.

   a. 2 Corinthians 3:5

   b. 2 Corinthians 4:7

   c. Philippians 2:13

   d. Philippians 3:3

7. Read and record Philippians 4:13.

   a. Where was Paul when he wrote this verse?

   b. What were his living conditions? (Philippians 1:13)

   c. Do you think he became discouraged at times?

   d. How would you feel if God called you into ministry, but you ended up in prison?

   e. With this in mind, what can you conclude about what Paul means by "all things"?

8. What is the hope of 1 Thessalonians 5:24?

9. Now go back and read all of Philippians 4 and note every reason for Paul's confidence.

Lesson Six—Cure for the Sagging Faith

1. Read 2 Timothy 4:7 and describe faith as a noun (object).

2. Read James 2:17-18 and describe faith as a verb (action).

3. In regard to your transformation, read Hebrews 11:1 and write it out in your own words.

4. Where does faith come from? (Ephesians 2:8)

5. Hebrews 11:6 says that we cannot please God without faith. Why do you think that is true?

6. Read the following and note what faith is essential for.

   a. Ephesians 2:8-9

   b. Ephesians 3:12

   c. Ephesians 3:17

   d. 1 Timothy 1:12

7. One reason we have little faith in people is because they change their minds and many times do not do what they promise. Look at the following verse and note how Jesus is different from people. (Hebrews 13:8)

8. All of us have bouts with doubts. Let's take a few minutes and focus on someone very close to Jesus who had questions of his own.

   a. Read Luke 1:39-44. What did the unborn child, John the Baptist, do when Mary walked into his mother's home?

b. Read John 1:29-34. What did John call Jesus? What did he hear God say?

c. How long had John known that Jesus was the Messiah? (Hint: Look back at a.)

d. Read Luke 7:18-28. Where was John at this time?

e. Why was he there? (Mark 6:17-18)

f. What were his disciples telling him?

g. What did he ask them to do?

h. What do you think caused John to doubt or question if Jesus was the Messiah, even though we have evidence that he had believed it before anyone else?

9. Sometimes our circumstances cause us to doubt God. Let's look at one final passage to see how God's timing is perfect. Read John 11:1-44.

a. Who was sick?

b. How did Jesus feel about him?

c. How long did Jesus wait before He went to Lazarus?

d. What happened in the meantime?

e. How long had he been in the tomb by the time Jesus arrived?

f. What would have begun to happen to Lazarus' body in that amount of time?

g. What happened when Jesus said, "Lazarus, come out"?

h. Was Jesus late?

i. Why did He wait?

j. What insight does this give you as to why God does not answer our prayers in our time frame?

k. Is He ever late? (Romans 15:13)

Lesson Seven—No More Stinkin' Thinkin'

1. Read Isaiah 26:3. Who will God keep in perfect peace?

2. Read Romans 8:5-8 and record everything you learn about the mind that thinks according to the Spirit and the mind that thinks according to the flesh.

3. On what are we to set our minds? (Colossians 3:1-2)

4. Read Isaiah 50:5-9. What do you think Isaiah meant by "set my face like flint"? How does this relate to Colossians 3:1-2?

5. What part do you think prayer plays in setting your mind? (Philippians 4:6-7)

6. Read Philippians 4:8 and make a list of what we are to think about. Beside each entry, write a word that represents the opposite thought. On a scale of one to ten, with ten being the positive thoughts and zero being the negative thoughts, how would you judge your thinking?

7. What does King David pray regarding his mind? (Psalm 26:2)

8. How does John describe Satan in John 8:44? How can this help you take every thought captive?

9. How did Satan influence Ananias in Acts 5:3?

10. Read 1 Peter 5:6-11.

   a. What is Satan doing now?

   b. What are we told to do?

   c. What will God do?

11. What is Satan's strategy? (2 Corinthians 11:12-15)

12. Let's go back to question number 1 in this lesson. The Amplified Version of the Bible is written with Hebrew definitions interwoven to help explain verses more clearly—amplified. I am going to give you Hebrew definitions of certain words in the verse.

   KEEP = *nasar*—to guard, protect, keep, used to denote guarding a vineyard and a fortress

   PEACE = *salom*—to be safe, be complete

   MIND = *yester*—to frame (like a picture), pattern, image, conception, imagination, thought, device

   STEADFAST = *samak*—to sustain, to be braced, to lean upon

   TRUST = *batach*—to attach oneself, to confide in, feel safe, be confident, secure

   Now, Hebrew scholar, write out an amplified version of Isaiah 26:3.

13. Read Colossians 3:15-16. The Greek word for "rule" is *brabeuo* and means "to act as an umpire." What is your understanding of how the peace of Christ can act as an umpire in your life?

Lesson Eight—Extending Grace—Receiving Freedom

We experience the ultimate makeover when we spend time in God's spa, but we also need to spend some time in God's gym.

1. Read and record 1 Timothy 4:7. The word "train" in the Greek is where we get the English word "gymnasium" and implies vigorous exercise. What parallels can you draw from training in godliness and working out in the gym?

2. Read and record Philippians 2:12-13. Remember, we are saved by grace—it is a gift. What do you think Paul means by "work out" your salvation? What are some exercises we can do for this workout?

3. One of the most strenuous exercises in the faith is forgiveness. Use a dictionary and define the word forgiveness.

4. What did Jesus teach about forgiveness in the following verses?

   a. Matthew 6:12

   b. Matthew 6:14-15

   c. Matthew 18:21-22

   d. Matthew 18:32-35

5. What did Paul teach about forgiveness?

   a. Ephesians 4:26-27

b. Ephesians 4:31-32

c. Colossians 3:13

6. Bitterness and unforgiveness can affect our physical appearance. Read Genesis 4:6-7.

a. What did God notice about Cain's appearance?

b. What was God's remedy?

c. What did God say would be the order of the change—doing and feeling?

7. What were Jesus' words on the cross recorded in Luke 23:34? Is there someone in your life who has hurt you that perhaps had no idea the pain they have caused? Could you pray the same prayer Jesus prayed on the cross?

8. Read and record John 13:17. So, where do you go from here?

Lesson Nine—Receiving God's Forgiveness

1. Read the following verses and note what they say about forgiveness of our sins.

a. Romans 5:1

b. Hebrews 10:10,14-22

2. Why did the Israelites not enter the Promised Land? (Hebrews 3:18-19)

3. If you do not believe God has forgiven you, what "Promised Land" might you not be able to enter this side of heaven?

4. Skim 2 Samuel 11 and 12.

   a. What was David's sin?

   b. What was the result of David's sin?

   c. How did he feel about it? (Psalm 51)

   d. How did God feel about David? (1 Samuel 13:14)

5. Read John 8:1-12.

   a. What did Jesus say *about* the woman caught in adultery?

   b. What did Jesus say *to* the woman caught in adultery?

   c. How did the sinful woman in Luke 7:36-50 feel about Jesus?

6. Many who struggle to forgive themselves feel unclean even though the Bible proclaims that they are clean (Romans 8:1). This reminds me of the salutation a person with leprosy had to make when they approached another person. They shouted "Unclean!" "Unclean!" In the story of the ten lepers recorded in Luke 17:11-19, when did their healing actually begin to take place? (verse 14)

7. Naaman was an army commander who had leprosy. Read his story in 2 Kings 5:1-19 and answer the following questions.

   a. To whom did he go for help?

b. What did Elisha tell him to do?

c. What was Naaman's initial reaction to these instructions?

d. How did his men convince him to obey?

e. What was the result of his obedience?

f. Have you ever felt that God's formula for forgiveness of your sins was too simple? Have you ever felt if it were more dramatic or severe, your forgiveness would be more believable?

g. What is the result of your obedience to accept God's solution to become clean?

h. What were Elijah's final words to Naaman? (verse 19)

Lesson Ten—Dressed for Success

1. Read each verse and note the attire of each person Satan attacked.

   a. Mark 14:52

   b. Luke 8:26-33

   c. Acts 19:13-16

2. While Satan desires to expose our shame, God desires to cover it. Read Zechariah 3:1-5 and note Joshua's change of wardrobe.

3. Look up the following verses and note what they say about our new wardrobe.

   a. Psalm 30:11

b. Romans 13:14

c. Galatians 3:27

d. Colossians 3:12

4. Read the following and note the significance of dressing in sackcloth.
   a. Genesis 37:33-34

   b. 1 Kings 21:17,27-28

   c. Esther 4:1

   d. Jeremiah 49:3

5. Read the following and note how God has changed our garments.
   a. Isaiah 61:1-3

   b. Isaiah 61:10

6. Do you tend to wear a garment of mourning or a garment of praise?

7. Do you tend to see yourself sitting in sackcloth and ashes with Tamar, or as a redeemed princess of the King? Are there any changes you need to make in your life to start walking in the truth of who you are?

8. What does John say is his greatest joy? (3 John 1:4)

Lesson Eleven—Putting Feet to Your Faith

1. Read Colossians 1:9-12 and note characteristics of a life "worthy of the Lord."

2. What does Jesus say follows our putting into action what we know to be true? (John 13:17)

3. Read Ephesians 5:3 and list some visible characteristics of walking in the flesh.

4. Read Galatians 5:22-23 and note some visible characteristics of walking in the Spirit.

5. Which is the greatest fruit of the Spirit? (1 Corinthians 13:13)

   a. If we passed each action through a filter of love, which characteristics of the flesh noted in question 3 would be eliminated?

   b. What is one of the greatest signs of maturity among believers? (1 John 5:3)

   c. When are we most like God? (1 John 4:17)

   d. When are others most likely to see God in us? (1 John 4:12)

   e. Would you say love is an action or an emotion?

6. How do we become mature? (Hebrews 5:14)

7. A big factor in overcoming the flesh is overcoming temptation. Look up the following verses and note what you learn about temptation.

   a. Why is Jesus able to help us when we are tempted? (Hebrews 2:17-18)

   b. How can He sympathize with our weakness? (Hebrews 4:15)

    c. How did Jesus instruct us to pray about temptation? (Matthew 6:13)

    d. Who is actually doing the tempting? (Luke 4:1-13; James 1:13-14)

    e. What does God promise to provide with each temptation? (1 Corinthians 10:13)

8. Read and record Romans 13:14.

    a. How do we make provisions for the flesh? (Think about what we see, where we go, etc.)

    b. Are there habits in your life that you need to change to "make no provision for" the flesh?

Lesson Twelve—Spending Time with the Beauty Artist

1. Read the following verses and notice what Jesus was doing. Also note what was going on before each.

    a. Matthew 16:13-19

    b. Mark 1:35

    c. Mark 6:46

2. Read Matthew 16:24-28 and Luke 9:23-27. How often are we told to "take up our cross and follow Jesus"?

3. How often did God provide manna for the Israelites wandering in the desert? (Exodus 16:4)

4. What is Jesus called in John 6:35?

5. Why were the disciples unable to cast out the demon in the following two accounts of the same incident? (Matthew 17:20; Mark 9:29)

6. Do you think time spent in prayer has an effect on the strength of our faith?

7. Let's spend some time examining Moses and his times at the spa with God.

   a. Read Exodus 20:19-20. What was the Israelites' response when God spoke directly to them?

   b. What did they say to Moses?

   c. On the other hand, how anxious was Moses to have God speak to him? (Exodus 34:28)

   d. How did God speak to Moses? (Exodus 33:11)

   e. What was Moses' one request? (Exodus 33:13)

   f. Moses also wanted to see God's glory. In order to prevent Moses from seeing God's face, where was he hidden? (Exodus 33:21-22)

   g. Where are you, as a child of God, now hidden? (Colossians 3:3)

   h. What is Jesus called in 1 Corinthians 10:4?

   i. What was the outward result of Moses' time at God's spa? (Exodus 34:29-30,35)

8. One way God speaks to us is through His Word. What does each of these verses say about the Word of God?

   a. Matthew 5:17-18

   b. 2 Timothy 3:16-17

   c. Hebrews 4:12

   d. 2 Peter 1:19-21

9. Read and record 2 Corinthians 4:16. How and when are we being renewed?

10. When is the best time for you to meet with God each day? What is the most conducive place?

Lesson Thirteen—Parting Words

As we share parting words, I want to focus on Jesus' parting words to His disciples and to us. Imagine a soldier going off to war who knows he will be placed on the front line of battle. The week before he's dispatched, he sits down to write his wife one final letter. He tries to include the essentials—how to continue in his absence, how to resist discouragement, and how much he loves and cherishes her. In John 14 through 17, Jesus reveals His heart to His disciples before He goes to the final battle at the cross.

1. Read John 14 and either mark or make a list of every word of instruction or encouragement. Then answer the following.

   a. Why should we not let our hearts be troubled?

b. Where was Jesus going and why was He going there?

c. How does a person get to the Father?

d. How does someone know what the Father is like?

e. Where did Jesus' words come from?

f. According to verse 12, what kinds of works is a Christian able to do?

g. What promise does Jesus make in verses 13 and 14?

h. How do we prove we love Jesus? (verses 15,21,23)

i. Who did Jesus send to be with us? (verse 16)

j. What are some names for the Holy Spirit?

k. What kind of hold did the prince of the world have on Jesus? (verse 30)

l. Why did Jesus go to the cross? (verse 31)

2. Read John 15:1-11 and note everything you learn about *remaining* or *abiding* in Christ.

3. Read John 17 and note what Jesus prayed for Christians then and now. How do we know His prayer is for us today?

4. Write a prayer of praise for what God has done in your life through this study.

Beauty Care Kit

Cleanser: "Wash away all my iniquity and cleanse me from my sin" (Psalm 51:2). "Because we have these promises, dear friends, let us cleanse ourselves from everything that can defile our body or spirit. And let us work toward complete purity because we fear God" (2 Corinthians 7:1 NLT).

Foundation: "No one can lay any foundation other than the one already laid, which is Jesus Christ" (1 Corinthians 3:11).

Blush: "Those who look to him are radiant; their faces are never covered with shame" (Psalm 34:5).

Eyes: "The commands of the LORD are radiant, giving light to the eyes" (Psalm 19:8).

Lips: "I will extol the LORD at all times; his praise will always be on my lips" (Psalm 34:1). "Because your love is better than life, my lips will glorify you" (Psalm 63:3).

Hair: "You anoint my head with oil; my cup overflows. Surely goodness and love will follow me all the days of my life" (Psalm 23:5-6). "Are not two sparrows sold for a penny? Yet not one of them will fall to the ground apart from the will of your Father. And even the very hairs of your head are all numbered.

So don't be afraid; you are worth more than many sparrows" (Matthew 10:29-31).

 Clothes: "For he [God] has clothed me with garments of salvation and arrayed me in a robe of righteousness" (Isaiah 61:10).

 Hands: "I will praise you as long as I live, and in your name I will lift up my hands" (Psalm 63:4). "I call to you, O LORD, every day; I spread out my hands to you" (Psalm 88:9).

 Feet: "How beautiful are the feet of those who bring good news!" (Romans 10:15). "Your word is a lamp to my feet and a light to my path" (Psalm 119:105).

 Perfume: "For we are a fragrance of Christ to God" (2 Corinthians 2:15 NASB).

Notes

Chapter One—A New Kind of Beauty

1. "Beauty Contest" by Carla Muir. Used by permission. Taken from Alice Gray, *More Stories for the Heart* (Sisters, OR: Multnomah Publishers, Inc., 1997).
2. Mimi Avins, "Teens Invest Heavily to Look Good,," *The Press Democrat,* Santa Rosa, CA, July 3, 2001, p. D1.

Chapter Two—The Great Cover-Up

1. Thomas Watson, *Gleanings from Thomas Watson* (Morgan, PA: Soli Deo Gloria Publications, 1995), p. 49.

Chapter Three—A Brand-New You

1. Charles Swindoll, *The Tale of the Tardy Oxcart* (Nashville, TN: W Publishing Group, 1998), p. 500.
2. Ibid., p. 503.
3. Neil T. Anderson and Robert L. Saucy, *The Common Made Holy* (Eugene, OR: Harvest House Publishers, 1997), p. 137.
4. The list of Scriptures in "My Identity with Christ" is adapted from "Who Am I?" taken from Neil T. Anderson, *Victory over the Darkness* (Ventura, CA: Regal Books, 1990), pp. 45-47.
5. Neil T. Anderson, *Victory over the Darkness* (Ventura, CA: Regal Books, 1990), p. 37.
6. Beth Moore, *Believing God* (Nashville, TN: LifeWay Christian Resources, 2004), p. 200.
7. Anderson and Saucy, *The Common Made Holy,* p. 39.

Chapter Four—Mirror, Mirror on the Wall

1. Neil T. Anderson and Robert L. Saucy, *The Common Made Holy* (Eugene, OR: Harvest House Publishers, 1997), p. 42.
2. *NIV Study Bible,* Kenneth Barker, general ed. (Grand Rapids, MI: Zondervan, 1995), p. 895.
3. Neil T. Anderson, *Living Free in Christ* (Ventura, CA: Regal Books, 1993), p. 72.
4. Anabel Gillham, *The Confident Woman* (Eugene, OR: Harvest House Publishers, 1993), pp. 111-12.

Chapter Five—Unshakable Confidence

1. Robert and Rosemary Barnes, *Rock Solid Marriage* (Grand Rapids, MI: Zondervan, 1996), p. 194.
2. Barbara Graham, "Shortcuts to Confidence," *Self,* July 1997, p. 116.
3. Alanna Nash, "Goldie Rules," *Good Housekeeping,* July 1997, p. 76.
4. Rebecca E. Greer, "Boost Your Confidence," *Woman's Day,* April 20, 1999, p. 29.
5. Kristen Kemp, "Confidence Makeovers," *YM,* April 2000, p. 24.
6. Susie Fields, "Super Confidence and How to Get It," *Salon Ovations,* September 1996, p. 30.
7. Ibid.
8. Ibid.
9. W.E. Vine, Merrill F. Unger, William White Jr., *Vine's Expository Dictionary of Old and New Testament Words* (Nashville, TN: Thomas Nelson, 1985), p. 1.
10. Neil T. Anderson, *Living Free in Christ* (Ventura, CA: Regal Books, 1993), p. 70.

Chapter Six—Faith Lift

1. Kenneth L. Barker and John R. Kohlenberger III, *Zondervan NIV Bible Commentary, Volume 2: New Testament* (Grand Rapids, MI: Zondervan, 1994), p. 9992.

2. Neil T. Anderson and Robert L. Saucy, *The Common Made Holy* (Eugene, OR: Harvest House Publishers, 1997), p. 283.

3. A.W. Tozer, *The Best of Tozer* (Grand Rapids, MI: Baker Book House, 1978), p. 120.

4. Oswald Chambers, *My Utmost for His Highest* (Grand Rapids, MI: Discovery House Publishers, 1992), May 30.

5. Taken from a sermon by Shadrack Meschack Lockridge. Despite their best efforts, the author and publisher were unable to locate the copyright holder of this material. If correction becomes necessary, proper notation will be given on future printing.

6. *NIV Study Bible,* Kenneth Barker, general ed. (Grand Rapids, MI: Zondervan, 1995), p. 1464.

7. Chambers, *My Utmost for His Highest,* June 5.

Chapter Seven—Renewed Mind

1. *NIV Study Bible,* Kenneth Barker, general ed. (Grand Rapids, MI: Zondervan, 1995), p. 12.

2. Beth Moore, *Breaking Free* (Nashville, TN: LifeWay Press, 1999), p. 184.

3. Ibid., p. 194.

4. Neil T. Anderson, *The Bondage Breaker* (Eugene, OR: Harvest House Publishers, 2006), p. 24.

5. Anabel Gilham, *The Confident Woman* (Eugene, OR: Harvest House Publishers, 1993), p. 97.

Chapter Eight—Exercise Regimen

1. Jean Lush, *Women and Stress* (Grand Rapids, MI: Revell, 1992), p. 113.

2. Kenneth L. Barker and John R. Kohlenberger III, *NIV Commentary* (Grand Rapids, MI: Zondervan Publishing House, 1994), p. 806.

3. Spiros Zodhiates, et al., eds., *The Complete Word Study Dictionary, New Testament* (Chattanooga, TN: AMG Publishers, 1992), p. 229.

4. Beth Moore, *Living Beyond Yourself* (Nashville, TN: LifeWay Press, 1998), p. 120.

5. Philip Yancey, *What's So Amazing About Grace?* (Grand Rapids, MI: Zondervan, 1997), pp. 98-99.

6. Corrie ten Boom, *Tramp for the Lord* (Grand Rapids, MI: Revell, 1974), pp. 83-86.

7. Ibid., p. 83.

8. Beth Moore, *Breaking Free* (Nashville, TN: LifeWay Press, 1999), p. 75.

9. Charles R. Swindoll, *Tale of the Tardy Oxcart* (Nashville, TN: W Publishing Group, 1998), p. 210.

Chapter Nine—Weight Loss Program

1. C.S. Lewis, *Mere Christianity* (Nashville, TN: Broadman and Holman Publishers, 1996), p. 104.

2. Henry Blackaby and Richard Blackaby, *Experiencing God Day-by-Day* (Nashville, TN: Broadman and Holman Publishers, 1997), p. 193.

3. Malcolm Smith, *Forgiveness* (Tulsa, OK: Pillar, 1992), pp. 6-7.

4. Charles R. Swindoll, *Joseph: From Pit to Pinnacle, Bible Study Guide* (Fullerton, CA: Insight for Living, 1982), p. i.

5. Beth Moore, *Breaking Free* (Nashville, TN: LifeWay Press, 1999), p. 84.

6. Ibid., p. 5.

7. Neil Anderson, *Victory over the Darkness* (Ventura, CA: Regal, 1990), p. 204.

8. David Seamands, *Healing for Damaged Emotions* (Wheaton, IL: Victor Books, 1981), pp. 310-32.

9. F.B. Meyer, *Devotional Commentary of Philippians* (Grand Rapids, MI: Kregel Publications, 1979), pp. 183-84.

Chapter Ten—A Brand-New Wardrobe

1. James Strong, from the *Hebrew and Chaldee Dictionary of Exhaustive Concordance of the Bible* (Nashville, TN: Holman Bible Publishers, n.d.), p. 58.

Chapter Eleven—Slough Off the Old

1. Neil Anderson and Robert Saucy, *The Common Made Holy* (Eugene, OR: Harvest House Publishers, 1997), pp. 315-16.

2. Peter H. Davids, *The Epistle of James* (Grand Rapids, MI: William B. Eerdmans Publishing Company, 1982), p. 161.

3. Neil Anderson, *Victory over the Darkness* (Ventura, CA: Regal, 1990), p. 85.

4. Ibid., p. 102.

Chapter Twelve—A Day at the Spa

1. Bruce Wilkerson, *Secrets of the Vine* (Sisters, OR: Multnomah Publishers, 2001), p. 109.

2. Henry Blackaby and Richard Blackaby, *Experiencing God Day-by-Day* (Nashville, TN: Broadman and Holman Publishers, 1997), p. 276.

3. Sharon Jaynes, *Becoming a Woman Who Listens to God* (Eugene, OR: Harvest House Publishers, 2004), p. 15.

4. A.W. Tozer, *Root of the Righteous* (Camp Hill, PA: Christian Publications, Inc., 1986), quote taken from chapter 29.

About the Author

Sharon Jaynes is an international inspirational speaker and Bible teacher for women's conferences and events. She is also the author of several books, including *"I'm Not Good Enough"...And Other Lies Women Tell Themselves; The Power of a Woman's Words; Becoming the Woman of His Dreams; Becoming a Woman Who Listens to God;* and *Your Scars Are Beautiful to God.* Her books have been translated into several foreign languages and impacted women all around the globe. Sharon and her husband, Steve, live in North Carolina and have one grown son, Steven.

Sharon is always honored to hear from her readers. Please write to her directly at: Sharon@sharonjaynes.com or at her mailing address:

Sharon Jaynes
P.O. Box 725
Matthews, North Carolina 28106

To learn more about Sharon's books and speaking ministry or to inquire about having Sharon speak at your next event, visit

www.SharonJaynes.com.

HARVEST HOUSE PUBLISHERS
EUGENE, OREGON

Other Books
by Sharon Jaynes

YOUR SCARS ARE BEAUTIFUL TO GOD
Sharon shares with women how emotional scars can lead to healing and restoration. Encouraging chapters and inspirational stories reveal how you can give your past pains over to the One who turns hurts into hope and heartache into happiness.

BUILDING AN EFFECTIVE WOMEN'S MINISTRY
This unique yet practical how-to manual offers a wide-range of help to women, from those just starting out to those who have a thriving ministry but could use a fresh idea or two. For groups large and small, this is a treasure trove of detailed information on how to serve and care for women.

BECOMING THE WOMAN OF HIS DREAMS
Sharon provides a thoughtful look at the wonderful, unique, and God-ordained role a woman has in her husband's life. If you would like a little "wow!" back in your relationship with the man you married, let seven simple secrets, biblical wisdom, and tender stories of both men and women inspire you to truly be the wife your husband longs for.

BECOMING A WOMAN WHO LISTENS TO GOD
"When I pore over the pages of Scripture," says Sharon, "I discover that some of God's most memorable messages were not delivered while men and women were away on a spiritual retreat, but right in the middle of the hustle and bustle of everyday life. He spoke to Moses while he was tending sheep, to Gideon while he was threshing wheat, to the woman at the well while she was drawing water for her housework. It is not a matter of does He speak, but will we listen." Discover with Sharon what it means to become a woman who listens to God.

A WOMAN'S SECRET TO A BALANCED LIFE
This essential book offers seven vital ways a Christian woman can prioritize her life more effectively: revere Jesus Christ as Lord; love, honor, and respect her husband; nurture her children; create a loving environment for family and friends; faithfully oversee time and money; mentor others; and extend herself to meet community needs.
Cowritten with Lysa TerKeurst.

HARVEST HOUSE PUBLISHERS
EUGENE, OREGON

To learn more about Harvest House books and
to read sample chapters, log on to our website:

www.harvesthousepublishers.com

HARVEST HOUSE PUBLISHERS
EUGENE, OREGON